DESIGN IN THE GARDEN

Inspiration · Design · Structure

HORTICULTURE
BOOKS

CINCINNATI, OHIO

DESIGN IN THE GARDEN

Inspiration · Design · Structure

Ursula Barth / Gary Rogers

A HORTICULTURE BOOK

Horticulture Publications, Boston, Massachusetts

First published in the US in 2004 ISBN 1-55870-735-2 paperback
Reprinted 2005
Originally published under the title *Gartenräume*
© 2003 by Deutsche Verlags-Anstalt GmbH, Stuttgart München

Horticulture is a subsidiary of F+W Publications Inc. Company
4700 East Galbraith Road, Cincinnati, OH 45236
1-800-289-0963

Printed in China by SNP Leefung
for Horticulture Publications, Boston, Massachusetts

Visit our website at www.hortmag.com

Desk Editor: Sarah Martin
Production Controller: Roger Lane

Contents

MATERIAL MATTERS

Styles and Moods

Design is a key factor in the impression we have of a particular space or room. Our perception of our surroundings and whether we feel at ease in them are largely determined by the shapes, colours and materials around us. The quality of a room, or an outdoor space, is revealed by whether it is used often and with pleasure. Good design relies on harmony, pleasing proportions and a successful choice of colour and materials, as well as on the creation of a suitable degree of tension.

The photographs on this page and the preceding ones show a variety of styles and how they create different moods, perhaps formal and geometrical, or maybe with a touch of the orient or fantastically colourful.

Stimulation for the Senses

Sight, hearing, smell, touch, taste – all five senses help us to understand the world around us and feel at home there, stimulating our emotions and enabling us to enjoy life.

▷ **Sight:** Such is our dependancy on vision that it is generally considered the most important of the senses. As a rule, the famous 'first impression' is essentially the visual one. Our positive, negative or indifferent judgements on the sights and scenes with which we are confronted on a daily basis are made both spontaneously and unconsciously. In a garden, a recurring theme, a well-realized design with pleasing proportions, a harmonious use of colour, an effective choice of materials and a skilful arrangement of plants can all determine whether what we see looks good.

▷ **Hearing:** A room's acoustics often decide whether we decide to remain in a room which we like the look of. Unfortunately, the acoustic factor is often neglected in garden design. Background sound effects are crucial to ensuring whether or not a garden actually provides the relaxing atmosphere it promises, helping us to forget the worries of the day. Acoustic pleasures in a garden can be many and varied – the twittering of birds, the gentle buzzing of bees, the quiet splashing or lively burbling of water, the rustling of leaves and branches in the wind – or just a calm stillness to give us time to pause and daydream.

▷ **Smell:** Fragrant perennials and flowering shrubs, aromatic herbs, the smell of warm earth, bark or freshly chopped wood – scents,

Top: These lush perennials, with their striking structure, are perfectly set off by the shimmering blue mirror formed by the pool of water.

Bottom: *A delicate, dream-like scene of subtle softness and fluidity, just asking to be approached. Foaming baby's breath (Gypsophila paniculata), white tulle and willows all seem to merge together.*

Right-hand page: *Different shapes and colours introduce an interesting tension in this scene. Particularly effective is the contrast between the metallic glint of the 'bed' of spheres and the matt wooden planks. Although plants play a secondary role in this compostion, this does not prevent it from being full of life. This is due in part to the lively interplay between light and shadow created by the tall bamboo canes, which may well have been expressly planned during the design process, even though its precise effect could not have been foreseen.*

fragrances and aromas enrich and enhance our experience of the outdoors. While scents or fragrances tend to emanate by themselves and hang in the air, aromas are released when leaves or bark are crushed underfoot, for example, and are often most distinct on warmer, sunnier days, particularly in secluded areas of the garden. Such aromas can be enhanced by objects that store heat and reflect the sunlight, such as stone walls.

▷ **Touch:** Interesting surfaces cry out to be touched and increase our perceptive skills, helping us to both feel and truly understand the world around us. Through our hands and skin, we can experience a vast range of sensations and surfaces: the feel of rugged or smooth stone, bark in all its countless varieties, smooth and bristly leaves, hard or soft leaves, the refreshing coolness of water, the natural warmth of wood, the pleasant heat emitted by sun-warmed stone and the alternation of cool shade and warm sunlight.

▷ **Taste:** Fruits and herbs are a welcome addition to any garden and make outdoor life complete; a pleasure for all the senses.

Handy hint
Scents and fragrances will enrich any garden. No seating area should be without its share of fragrant plants, since it will be the perfect place to enjoy all the different perfumes in all their glory. A sheltered spot can only increase the intensity of their fragrance.

The Leading Players and the Supporting Cast

Any garden is formed of several or many different elements – gardens are a fusion of all the shapes, colours, structures, plants and materials used to create them. To judge a whole garden on a single horticultural aspect – good or bad – is pointless because a successful garden captivates us through the interplay of its plants and through the effect of a well-chosen variety of inanimate materials – the hard landscaping. Each individual element has a different role in proceedings – as in a play, there should be a sprinkling of leading actors and an array of supporting cast, all playing an important part in the overall effect. This applies to the garden as a whole, as well as to the materials used to construct the various paths, patios, seating areas, walls, steps, pergolas, fences or furniture. Materials chosen for these items must do justice to the overall design, but should also look good in their own right.

Personal taste, the desired effect and the size of the garden will determine whether you use a single material consistently in the design or select a suitable combination. It is worth bearing in mind that larger gardens can tolerate more variety than their smaller counterparts. In the latter, one or two materials will suffice for surfaces, walls or steps, and look better than too much variation, which will only succeed in making what was already a small space look even smaller and rather cluttered. In addition, in a small garden, stark contrasts have a disruptive effect, while larger spaces can absorb more contrasts and eyecatching effects, especially when the garden is subdivided into separate, independent areas. As

long as the garden is unified by a theme linking the different elements, such contrasts will make it seem especially invigorating and full of life.

A variety of styles

The theme you use in designing your garden is determined by personal preference. In the past, the emphasis was often placed on current trends – both in gardens and in architecture – which meant that you would often come across similar, recurring features. Victorian terraced houses are a good example of a rigid, albeit effective, architectural design style. Today, we have access to a huge range of styles and can simply chose what we like best. Gardens are tailored to suit their owners' taste: classic or modern, it is entirely up to the designer. Those who like to be close to nature can create an informal, unstructured design and plant their beds with native plants; alternatively, if you like definite forms and clearer contours, you would be better to opt of a more formal style. Designs

Right-hand page, top: *A picture of harmony. This attractive gravel path cuts a swathe through the beds with its neat and sturdy edging stones. The white arches, around which pink roses engagingly entwine themselves, add the perfect finishing touch.*

Right-hand page, bottom: *Summer splendour. In summer, plants, along with supporting hard landscaping, are such a delight – especially when they incorporate a magnificent water feature such as this one, which has been made with a variety of materials.*

modelled on garden styles from the past are just as effective as themed garden creations, and foreign designs, whether Japanese, English or Mediterranean, can also act as an inspiration. Every type of design has its merits, provided, of course, that it suits its surroundings.

The right material

While form and shape determine the basic design, the materials make a decisive contribution, giving the design much of its final character. There are no foolproof methods or formulas for chosing the right materials. Nevertheless, a few general guidelines should be kept in mind.

▷ House and garden are inseparable partners and should always be treated as such. The materials used in the garden must always complement those used for the house, and the same applies to colour. It is even possible for the forms, structures and proportions used for the house to be reflected in the space around it.

▷ Inside and outside can be made to blend into one through the use of identical materials. For example, a natural stone floor in the living room can continue outside on to the patio, the two separated only by the panes of the French windows. Alternatively, a wooden-style interior can be reflected in the natural surroundings outside. If the materials used are the same, this will make the entire visible area seem larger.

▷ Materials from your local area are likely to suit your garden best. Gardens fit in particularly well with their surroundings when stone and other products from the same region are used in their construction. The only exceptions to this rule are city gardens where there are often many different materials in the surrounding area, making it impossible and unnecessary to choose something that is entirely in keeping.

Design materials are crucial to creating a pleasing effect. However, they should never be allowed to take over, but rather slot seamlessly into the whole ensemble. This does not prevent them from being eyecatching, either in their own right or by helping to reinforce a style or ambience.

Pictures and frames

Gardens often act as refuges, reflecting the dreams, ideas and desires of their owners. Yet they are rarely isolated and utterly independent of their surroundings. Your own private space may be right next to some public land or your neighbour's property, and the transitional areas in between can set the tone of an area. It follows that it is crucial to take great care when you are planning the framework for your garden: that part of it which will link it into its surroundings. The old adage that the whole is always more than the sum of its parts is so true in this case. For example, it is rarely a good idea to make hedges and fences, in particular, as well as flowerbeds that are visible from outside the property, too striking or overwhelming – and it isn't very fair on your neighbours either. Similarity can create harmony and a sense of identity, and is not necessarily synonymous with 'sameness' in a negative sense. There is always room for individuality, in the detailing, for example, and in secluded areas. As a rule, this individuality is most effective near the house itself. Generally, the further you are from buildings, especially if your garden backs on to open ground, the less distinct and more subtle the transition from the garden to the surrounding area needs to be. Striking, exotic shrubs with colourful foliage should be used as carefully here as shapes, colours and materials that do not come from your area. They can certainly be used to provide a surprising and eyecatching finishing touch, but wider use should be confined to private, less publicly visible areas of your garden.

Constancy and change

A huge advantage of outdoor spaces is their diversity and adaptability: the decor is in a constant state of flux. The garden changes along with the seasons, beginning with the long-awaited spring awakening before proceeding to the lush green and the exuberant flower displays of summer; followed by the more subdued tones of autumn, which in turn give way to the relative sparseness and sombreness of winter.

A lasting structural framework for these seasonal changes is usually provided by the garden's hard landscaping, which comes to the fore during the winter months, when its shapes become more striking. It lends the garden a certain stability and moulds it through the decades. Time is a crucial element in the development of a garden as the plants mature in their respective positions, often greatly altering the general appearance of the scene, but it does not have as much effect on the garden's more static elements.

COLOUR AND LIGHT

Colour in the Limelight

Of the many things that attract our attention in the garden, colour is the one which has the most immediate effect on our mood. Colours have the power to make us feel at ease or to unsettle us. Garden design can only be successful if sufficient attention is paid to their choice and arrangement. So they are clearly one of the key factors to take into account when planning a garden, closely followed by light and shadow (see pages 16–17).

Similar colours, like blue and green, influence each other in the effect they have and the way we perceive them. The blue in this example (left-hand page) acts as a frame for the plants, while powerful shades of pink (see above) can dominate an entire space. Such spectacles as this are more suitable for brief seasonal displays than for lasting arrangements.

The Phenomenon of Colour

Some knowledge of colour theory is indispensable for making successful designs with colours and their combinations, as well as their correct use in both light and shade.

Colour is something we take for granted, but most of us would have difficulty if asked to define it. For colour is intangible: although real, it is hard to describe in words. We see colour through our eyes, which then produce impulses in the brain so that we understand what we see. For colour to be visible, light must be present: without light there is no colour. Our perception of colour depends on the actual quality of the light. We can only see so-called 'true' colours in white light, which contains all the colours in the spectrum. As a rule, daylight is not fully 'white', but instead consists of different, fluctuating colour particles, the most dominant of which take over and influence all the others. For example, the same scene can appear completely different according to the time of day or the amount of sunlight. Imagine harsh midday sunlight (yellow) in comparison with a reddish evening light or a hazy blue morning light. Bright sunlight is itself such a glaring yellow that only the strongest of colours can make an impact under its shine. In the shade everything blends and merges into tones of grey-violet, with the effect that only bright colours like white or yellow have a chance to shine out.

An object is the colour it reflects, absorbing as it does the other colour particles present in the light. This is how leaves, for example, gain their greenness, as their pigment, chlorophyll, reflects green. We see white only when all colour particles are reflected by an object; while black is seen when none of the colours are reflected. When you try to judge the effect of colour in an object, don't underestimate the importance of its surface. An object's texture determines whether we perceive the colour as matt or glossy. The smoother and shinier the surface, the brighter the colour, while rough or hairy surfaces disturb the reflected light and result in a more matt colouring.

A colourful education

Current colour theory uses the colour wheel, containing the primary colours (red, blue, yellow) and the secondary colours (green, purple, orange), which are derived from them and are placed between them on the wheel. These colours are closely related and can influence one another, either by increasing their intensity or softening it.

The brain has a habit of linking a colour with its opposite number on the colour wheel, which is why we experience a type of purple double-vision after looking directly into the yellow sun. Such opposing colour pairs create what are called 'complementary contrasts'. Yellow and purple, blue and orange, and red and green produce these effects.

'Simultaneous contrast' is where closely related colour pairs (those that are near each other on the colour wheel) influence each other, even eclipsing one another to a certain extent. As a

Left-hand page, top: *Blue tones. The neutral green of the leaves links the yellow and blue. The open-work iron gate ensures that the strength of the blue is subtly underplayed.*

Left-hand page, bottom: *Creating effects with warm colours. Colour progressions using colours with similar pigmentation result in a harmonious whole.*

Top: *Effective contrast. Although this row of white trunks is perceived as a continuous band or surface, the spaces in between mean that it still seems airy and light.*

Bottom: *An eye-catching effect. The bright yellow of this garden gate boldly declares its presence. The combination of the powerful yellow and light violet is potentially strident, and probably best confined to individual features like this which are meant to stand out in your garden.*

result, such colour pairs appear to drift away from one another. If the adjacent colours already complement each other, then of course their tones do not change; in fact each enhances the effect of the other.

Colours are not always analysed using the colour wheel, but can also be graphically presented within the ribbon-shaped colour spectrum depicting all colours discernible to the human eye, from red (short wave) through orange, yellow, green and blue to violet (long wave) — all the colours of the rainbow, in fact.

Garden furniture can be eyecatching too. The best effects are created where the background is tranquil, as in this example with its peaceful green backdrop.

Right-hand page, top: Cool impressions. Blue and purple play the leading roles in this garden. White separates them, making them stand out all the more. The contrast between the two colours sets the tone of the garden and demands the observer's complete attention; the green of the lawn is of secondary importance, being hardly visible.

Right-hand page, bottom: The power of light. In the garden, planning with colour also entails planning with light. While bright sunlight emphasizes the contrast between white and green, with each colour sharply distinguished from the other, shadow blurs the two and they merge in the half-light.

Theoretically, these colours are always considered separately, whereas in reality the fluid nature of colour prevents such a clear-cut approach. The colours in the spectrum are defined as 'shades': the pure colour, without the addition of black, white or grey. However, pure colours are rare, and so 'colour value' is used to describe the way in which the shades can be altered through the addition of black (darkening) or white (lightening).

The colour value of pure colours can vary. Yellow notches up the highest amount, while purple brings up the rear. This means that yellow is the ideal candidate for being made darker but cannot be lightened to any great extent. While purple is the opposite. Finally, 'colour intensity' or 'saturation' refers to the amount of grey that is contained within a particular colour.

The effect of colour

Apart from creating moods, colours can also have an immediate effect on the way we perceive the surrounding space. This is not surprising, bearing in mind that we notice colours long before we see any abstract shapes. A careful choice of colour can give the illusion of increased space, depth and distance, and it can also create a feeling of proximity, lightness and brightness or weight and prominence. The use of colour is a major contributor to whether we find a space peaceful and relaxing or whether it stimulates and excites our senses.

Here are a few basic rules that are easy to remember and put into practice.

▷ Cooler colours generate an impression of depth and distance, namely all shades of blue and purple, grey and, to a certain extent, brown.

▷ Paler background shades of the colour used in the foreground can create a similar feeling of increased space.

▷ Warm colours – yellow, orange and red – make objects stand out and seem sharper, and they reduce the feeling of depth.

▷ These effects of cold and warm colours are also responsible for the fact that objects seem more clearly defined in warm light, standing out

Handy hint

How intensely we perceive a particular colour largely depends on the way it is displayed. A strong colour, used in a flat, two-dimensional way, can seem too 'in your face'. However, if given an extra dimension, perhaps with a latticed fence or a display of flowers, its dominance can be lessened.

more than when seen in a colder light with a bluer, cooler tint.

▷ White, which contains all the colours of the spectrum, is thought of as a neutral shade, and is perfect for separating different colours and toning down the effects they have on each other. It also functions well as a mediator, reducing the sometimes excessively stark contrast between strong and pure colours.

▷ Grey is capable of assuming a similar function, even though, unlike white, it is easily influenced by the contrasting colour of its neighbour. Grey makes strong colours brighter and enlivens pastel tones.

▷ Green can also mediate between colours in the garden, seeming neutral, particularly in the open air, fading into the background and giving way to the striking contrasts of other colours. Personal taste determines the colours we like and will therefore use most in the garden. Nevertheless, it is important to consider the effect that colours have on our moods. Everyone has likes and dislikes and favourite colours, but certain colours have recognized effects, and they can and should be consciously used to influence the ambience and to help achieve a particular atmosphere.

Blue is far and away the most popular colour with both men and women and it has many positive associations: harmony, trust, peace, sympathy and friendship. At the same time, it is also linked with eternity, expanse and yearning. And its tendency to blur contours further

Nocturnal designs. Detached from their background, the dispersed yellow lines of these trees appear to float in the black night, creating a dramatic scene of colour and light.

24

underscores its versatility. **Red** is next on the list of most popular colours. Associated with warmth, heat, passion, excitement, spontaneity and eroticism, it tends to hog the limelight.

Green, on the other hand, is always seen as a soothing colour. It symbolizes nature, life, freshness, springtime and hope.

Yellow will always be linked with the sun, with light and warmth, whereas **purple** has a more magical, mysterious effect; and for the more gentle and sensitive among us there is delicate **pink.**

Black and **white** are always seen as being in conflict. While the former stands for loneliness and sorrow but also objectivity and functionality, we associate the latter with purity, innocence and perfection. Whereas white is generally looked upon positively, opinion is often divided on the appropriateness of black.

Colour combinations

People who have a good feeling for colour can combine suitable shades without even thinking about it. However, we are not all fortunate enough to have this talent. So the rest of us should refer back to the cardinal rules of colour theory when we begin planning our gardens.

One successful way to combine colours is to use **complementary colour contrasts** – in other words to use colour pairs that are positioned opposite one another on the colour wheel, such as orange and blue. Each of these enhances the effect of the other and because of this, such colour combinations are particularly intense, and almost glowing. However, some of these combinations can be too extreme, especially in the case of particularly strong or pure colours. To make them more acceptable, they can be lightened or darkened; the lighter shade always being made even lighter and the darker one darker. For example, yellow and purple would be most successful changed to pastel yellow and dark purple, rather than to dark yellow and delicate violet.

About colour. Colours attract the most attention when they are presented two-dimensionally and unchallenged by any other shade. This makes their many qualities become apparent, and has an immediate effect on our senses and mood. However, it is worth considering whether using just one colour is more appropriate for any particular design. Below, soothing shades of blue and purple allow for more flexibility than, for example, stirring, deep reds. In general, it is better to limit designs that use one colour to specific areas of the garden. This means that you have to seek them out, and this ensures that the effect remains out of the ordinary.

Another popular method is to use **colour triads**, in which three opposite colours on the colour wheel are chosen, resulting in combinations such as yellow-blue-red or orange-purple-green. The often excessively garish contrasts that result can be made more acceptable by lightening each colour to a pastel shade.

Colour progressions involve choosing a single section on the colour wheel and including all its different tones. These designs always look good because they contain lots of colours with similar pigments, creating a feeling of harmony.

Your taste and what you want to achieve in your garden will decide whether you use only warm, yellow-red tones, say, or just colder, blue-purple ones, or whether you think a transitional approach, moving from warmer to cooler shades, is more appropriate. Colour progressions using just one colour often have the most subtle effect. Nevertheless, it is crucial that you are aware that this approach means that garden, and gardener, are more or less at the mercy of a single colour and the moods and emotions it releases in you – achieving a really satisfactory result with this method can be difficult.

Handy hint
Powerful colours are often difficult to use, but they can be effective rather than oppressive if they are surrounded by larger areas of paler pastel-shaded surfaces of either the same or a matching shade.

WOOD – WARM, SENSUAL AND TRANSIENT

Making the Most of Wood

Wood radiates warmth and life, and it is these characteristics
that distinguish it from all other landscaping materials. It can
easily be made into many different shapes, and its longevity
can be increased and its appearance enhanced by applying a
range of paints, stains or preservatives. It is extremely valuable
for its versatility, whether you want to have a smart paling
fence (see pages 28–29), decorative wood pile (left-hand
page) or snug patio (above).

Choosing and Using Wood

Wood is one of the most popular materials for both house and garden, principally due to the fact that it radiates a warm feeling and also feels warm to the touch. While stone, brick or concrete paving take a while to heat up in the sun before they are pleasant to walk on with bare feet, you do not have to wait long before you can walk on wood without feeling the cold. Wood is so tactile; it invites us to stroke it, enjoying its contours, textures and irregularities and exploring its character, again and again. If it is freshly chopped, it can also awaken our sense of smell, intensifying the garden experience. Although the intense, earthy aroma does disappear, more quickly in the case of some types of wood than others, it makes a deep impression on the senses and stays in our minds, being quickly remembered and very evocative of time and place.

As wood is an organic and natural building material, it blends in perfectly with the rest of the natural environment; its ability to harmonize with plants and the natural surroundings of the garden and the wider area is unsurpassed. However, it is subject to decay and its appearance and work as a garden building material – whether fencing, trellis pergola or decking – can only be expected to be sustained for a certain amount of time.

Which wood?

In the open air, wood is permanently exposed to the elements, so it will inevitably suffer weathering and, in the end, will be destroyed. In some ways, this is an accepted part of using wood, and when we put it in our gardens, we know that eventually it will need to be renewed. However, most of us do not want to have to keep rebuilding complex structures. Unfortunately, many of our native woods are unsuitable for use outside because they are too scarce, too weak or just don't last for long enough. Those species with the best defences against decay – oak, beech and sweet chestnut – are more expensive and in short supply. And those that can cope with being exposed to the elements and that are strong enough – the various pines, not all native – are still susceptible to fungi and insects – in other words, without help, they decay relatively quickly.

Insects and fungi are not the only problems that the more affordable varieties of timber suffer from: Douglas fir, spruce and other softwoods have a tendency to develop blue patches of discoloration. The best way to disguise this is through painting or staining.

Exotic woods like teak, bongossi, kambala and merbau and the North American western red cedar are superior to our native varieties in terms of longevity and wear. However, there are some big disadvantages related to their use. First and foremost is the problem of sustainability: you should only use these woods if you can be sure your supplier obtained them from an ecologically managed plantation rather than from the over-exploited rainforests. And then there is the price: because they are imported from a long way away, most are much

Page 32, top: *The ways in which wood can be used are many and varied. However, where possible, avoid direct contact between the wood and the earth.*

Page 32, centre: *A woven fence with a difference. A fence like this, constructed solely from rustic, unstripped rounded wooden poles, is best suited to rural locations.*

Page 32, bottom: *Wood is also suitable for walking on, as shown in this innovative mosaic pathway. However, avoid using it for paths that experience heavy use, and be very careful when you walk on it in wet weather as it does become slippery.*

Right: *A testimony to creativity. Artistic joinery work like this is generally only to be found in historic gardens. Leafy walkways, pergolas and pavilions are worthy of the term 'architecture' and enrich old-fashioned gardens like this one. Often lasting for over a hundred years, this type of construction is proof of wood's enduring qualities in the open air, provided that it is properly maintained.*

more expensive than home-grown or continental timbers. Finally, there is the fact that they are not 'native', so gardeners who want to be in keeping with their environment may prefer to stick with indigenous timber, anyway. One of the main problems with softwoods – their tendency to rot – can be avoided by buying pressure-treated timber and also ensuring that water can easily run off any

construction and that the wood will not receive any permanent or regular soaking – such as from a hose or drainpipe – apart from the, obviously, unavoidable rain.

Unfortunately, pressure treatments tend to dye the wood so it is often necessary to add paint or a stain on top, which means that you won't have a natural finish. In addition, there are questions about the safety of pressure treatments and waterproofing. The chemicals used come under the definition of hazardous waste, and cannot be recycled.

In the end, it is down to personal taste, budget and your conscience – as well as availability.

Natural or coloured?

Untreated wood will always be the first choice for those who love wood's natural character. Over time and exposure to the elements, some woods develop an attractive silvery-grey sheen that helps them to blend wonderfully into their environment. However, if you want to make a construction stand out from its surroundings or really catch the eye, you will need to add a coat of paint. You can choose between porous-type stains, which leave the wood's structure and grain visible, and thicker paints and varnishes, which can be either matt or glossy. Whatever you choose – stains, paints and varnishes – all have to be reapplied on a regular basis – as often as every two years. If they are acting as a waterproof layer and become damaged then they must be reapplied as soon as possible.

These wooden steps seem to merge into one with their side-planting of Cotoneaster dammeri. Although the result is undeniably picturesque, wood is not always suitable for outdoor steps as it can be slippery. If the flight of steps is long, as here, and there is no handrail, a quiet walk through the garden might become a dangerous adventure!

If you do decide to paint the wood, try to use environmentally-friendly paints. Consult the packaging for more information.

The link between style and function

Wood is incredibly versatile and it can take on many different styles and guises. Take just one example – sawn wood. There is a wide choice of finish alone: planed, sanded, painted or even left coarse (it is always possible to smooth the edges to avoid splinters). Then, with the simple addition of grooves, boards and thicker planks can be made suitable for decking – further proof of wood's flexibility. For those who like a more natural treatment, unstripped logs can be laid along the edge of flowerbeds to make attractive borders, and unstripped branches can be woven into fences; while for more traditional garden settings, formal planed-wood structures are best. For those who prefer intricate designs, many woods can also be carved. In short – wood can be rustic and coarse, but at the same time elegant and modern: it is entirely up to the gardener.
Some ideas for using wood:

▷ Fences and gates – can be rustic or formal.
▷ Greenhouses, pavilions and furniture – usually better made with planed wood, although rustic benches look good in the right setting.
▷ Pergolas, trellises and archs – again, rustic or formal.
▷ Decking – planed, grooved wood is the most common material used.

Wood is not ideal for steps as it is too slippery when wet. Nor it is recommended for use in retaining walls as it rots too quickly, although you will get several years service from treated ex-railway sleepers.

Handy hint
As a surface for pathways, wood should be confined to stretches that are not in constant use. There is an alternative, which is again made of wood: bark chippings make a safe and attractive path surface.

House and garden as one. Colour co-ordinated wooden planks are used in this patio and the wooden decking in the garden, successfully linking the building with the surrounding area.

Eyecatching layout. Here, wood and gravel are combined to form a pleasingly structured path. A simple idea used to great effect. A practical feature is the gravel's ability to drain water, preventing the wood from remaining wet.

A country garden path. Simple wooden boards point the way. This path is flexible and easy to replace. A thin layer of gravel or stone chippings underneath protects the wood from the damp soil below.

Sweeping contours. It is rare to see bark used in such a creative way. Set on end, it forms an attractive border for this vegetable patch, and prevents the soil from spilling onto the path. It is beautifully set off by the chipping path.

Top: *Climate change. Unlike in our own damp climate, wood is a suitable material for outdoor steps in the Mediterranean area, due to the relative lack of rain. The uneven nature of this flight of steps, and its accompanying planting, lends it a sense of whimsy.*

Centre: *Bark chippings make an economical and practical path surface, best used for paths in shaded areas of the garden which are less likely to dry out. Among its advantages is that it is pleasantly soft, easily absorbing your footsteps.*

Bottom: *Wooden surfacing can be produced using either round or rectangular cuts of wood. The advantage of the rounded variety is that little plants can grow in the gaps. As with all wood surfaces, it is crucial to install a gravel foundation to increase water drainage.*

Just wood. Despite being made almost exclusively from wood, this roof garden appears anything but rustic, largely as a result of its ornate finish. The overall effect is comfortable and cheerful with an elegant air. The garden's restrained colour scheme, which is limited to light brown and green with a touch of zinc, makes the small space appear larger.

Fences and Gates – Beautiful Boundaries

Left: *Bench and gate unify this garden scene. The simple white lacquered wooden gate fills a gap in the high green hedge, while the bench attracts our attention. Together these elements have a dual function: they ensure the privacy of the garden's occupants and yet arouse our curiosity, encouraging us to speculate on what might be found inside.*

Above: *Simple wooden paling fences are often used to enclose country gardens. The use of climbing plants and bushes over this one has obscured the boundary and the colourful flower display invites you to peer over.*

Fences: Variations on a Theme

Fences have a firm foothold in the history of the garden. Their original purpose was to protect a piece of cultivated land, which had been painstakingly created from the wilderness, from animals that were likely to destroy the crops. Nowadays, few of us need to worry about wild animals when we plan ways in which to enclose our plots. However, fences and boundaries do play a variety of roles in the garden; they should be able to keep both stray animals and unwanted intruders at bay, and also separate public and private land. Most property owners want it to be clear where their land begins and ends. It goes without saying that every type of enclosure tells you a great deal about its architect – a bit like a first impression.

Consider your neighbours

When you plan your fence, the first thing you must do is to take into account the view over the fence. Next, consider the boundaries where public and private property are linked or your garden is attached to a neighbours' one. You can get some good ideas for suitable fencing by thinking about the layout of the surroundings and the character of the district in general, and, of course, taking into account your neighbours' wishes. One of the reasons why many villages are so pretty is the way the different gardens are separated from each other in individual and attractive ways. However, in places where there is a hotchpotch of different types of fences, walls, materials and colours and too little greenery, the effect is anything but restful and can be off-

Top: *The rustic touch. This simple fence of rounded wooden poles is reminiscent of the boundary of a paddock or field. The exceptionally tall posts create an unusually rhythmic effect, successfully offsetting the striking horizontal structure. Fences such as these are best suited to larger plots and should really only be used to connect gardens or fields to open countryside.*

Bottom: *Asian flair. Bamboo canes lend western gardens an oriental ambience. Here they have been used to create an imposing screen and plant support. Because bamboo is long-lasting and comes in a variety of sizes and colours, it can be used to make many unusual, attractive constructions.*

Top: *Internal structure. In larger gardens such as this, fences prove invaluable in separating and emphasizing different spaces and features. Here, the gleaming white of the fence constrasts well with the green foliage and the magenta roses. These provide the fence with a green base, ensuring it blends seamlessly into the scene as a whole.*

Bottom: *Aged with dignity. Natural materials often become more beautiful through weathering. Allowing this to happen is not a sign of neglect, but instead shows respect for the original materials and construction. To achieve this kind of ageing effect, use untreated wood.*

putting rather than inviting. Here are a few factors to bear in mind for your boundaries.

▷ Using similar colours, designs and materials creates a feeling of harmony, space and identity in streets, housing estates or even towns – think of an archetypal Cotswold village, for example.

▷ Individuality is important and desirable, and can add detail and variety to a theme.

▷ Fences and greenery belong together. Plants enliven inanimate structures and create inviting transitional zones, welcoming visitors. Ideally, fences should have a strip of lawn or greenery in front of them.

▷ Fences should never be higher than necessary and as a rule should not exceed 90–100cm (about 3ft). If a fence is over 1.2m (4ft), it turns turn into an off-putting barrier.

▷ Consider the impact your fence will have on the many small animals, such as hedgehogs, that might like to visit your garden – it might be a good idea to leave some gaps so that they can get in and out easily.

▷ During the design process, think about both the inside and the outside of the garden. Inside the garden, fences should create a feeling of security, maybe also protecting against the wind, keeping away unwanted observers and reducing noise. Seen from the outside, they define the boundary, also acting as decoration and as a kind of welcome to both house and garden.

▷ Always check the legalities before starting to design or build a fence or wall, as it may be necessary to get planning permission. For further details, contact your local council.

Top: Gates have a seemingly contradictory double function. On the one hand, they enclose a given space, marking it out and controlling access to it. On the other hand, they welcome visitors, granting them access to this same space. They can either recede modestly into their surroundings, catching the eye only on closer inspection, or form a striking feature, clearly marking out entrances. They work best, however, when they fit in with their surroundings, harmonizing with fences, walls and hedges. Slatted gates such as these give only a hint of what lies hidden behind, making us curious to discover the sights eluding our gaze.

Bottom: A charming decoy. Decorative effects are highly desirable on fences, too.

Traditional forms

Wood is the most popular material for building fences. There is an enormous variety, in all kinds of shapes, colours and styles.

Paling fences are ideal for natural gardens that are intended to blend in with the countryside. They are made from roughly split wooden stakes, stripped or unstripped, and not planed in any way. They are often chestnut wood, but similar natural-looking fences can be made from young, unstripped spruce or pine.

Picket fences are another variation, which are more suitable for an urban environment. They are made from planed slats.

Prefabricated panelled fences, such as woven, closeboarded and wavy-edged (larch-lap) are all cheap and readily available. They are long-lasting and serviceable, but not always beautiful. Unfortunately, they are also often stained an unattractive red-brown colour and will need to be repainted to blend in with most gardens.

Handy hint

Integrate your fences into the garden by using plants that wind themselves around the wood, such as honeysuckle or vines. Suitably sized shrubs planted behind the fence also fit the bill. However, if you require a more open and lighter effect, a base of low-growing perennials is ideal. Alternatively, less vigorous twining climbing plants such as clematis, hops, sweet peas, morning glory, nasturtiums or black-eyed Susan would also do nicely.

While side entrances and driveways are often better when they merge seamlessly with their surroundings, main entrances should be consciously designed to catch the eye. This way they provide a formal invitation to enter the space they protect.

Reeds can be used to make attractive fences and create an air of privacy. In this example, they are piled loosely between vertical wooden posts, to give a natural, unforced effect that is tropical in ambience. Although reeds and other rigid grasses, such as bamboo, are not suitable for weaving due to their brittleness, they can be tied up in bundles or worked into matting to good effect.

Wickerwork

Willow and hazel canes can be used to give the garden a natural feel. Traditionally, they are made into wicker fences by weaving together the still-flexible shoots, and as such they do provide effective garden enclosures. Unfortunately, although beautiful, they are relatively short-lived and soon succumb to the elements of weather and time. For this reason, they are better used as internal space dividers rather than to fence off the boundaries to your property.

'Living' fences will provide pleasure for longer. These are made from living willow canes that are planted into the soil and then woven into a luxuriantly sprouting interlacing network as they grow. Suitable species include the common osier (*Salix viminalis*) and purple osier (*Salix purpurea*). There are plenty of suppliers of willow canes and most will provide you with the information you need to get started. The best time for fence weaving is in spring when active growth is under way. Store the pre-cut canes in water until you are ready to plant them into the soil. Fences are not the only popular form of wickerwork. Wicker tunnels, igloos and tepees have become an integral part of natural garden settings, while hazel and willow bowers are used to create places of seclusion and rest in the garden.

In some areas, hedge laying is popular. This involves establishing hedges of hazel and other plants. Every few years, these hedges are managed by slicing partway through the upward-growing branches, then bending these down and weaving them through adjacent stems to form a thick inpenetrable barrier. Because the stems are only part-sliced, they go on growing.

Above: *A nod to tradition. Hurdles were formerly used to enclose pastures. Today, they effectively shut off the garden from unwanted observers, while retaining their original visual appeal.*

Below: *Fluid transitions. This open wicker fence purports to separate the meadow from the flower garden. However, those plants making a bold attempt to escape into the neighbouring terrain ensure that the dividing line becomes hard to pin down!*

Garden Features – Essential and Eyecatching

Left: *Every detail of this pergola has been designed using one of the most basic geometric forms, the square. Its connection with the house is a logical extension of this formal theme. With its clear, restful straight lines, the pergola creates an unusual high-quality space; the light brown natural wood adds warmth, and the trelliswork creates an acceptable compromise between privacy and transparency. In the course of time, climbing plants will take over and blur the outlines of this airy construction.*
Right: *In more secluded areas of the garden, arbours such as this one are an eyecatching feature in themselves. From them you can observe all the other goings-on in peace and quiet, viewing the sights and colours and experiencing the moods of the garden from a completely different perspective.*

A Room with a View

Above: *Hide and seek.. This rustic bench sits discreetly beneath the pergola. The luxuriantly entwined wisteria 'roof' adds to the enchantment of the scene. Round, unstripped wooden posts underline the character of this retreat.*

A pretty detail. Pergola supports are generally joined with nails or screws yet here the rounded beams are bound together with a rope of natural fibres. Although this requires some skill, the attractive result repays all the hard work!

Seating areas, where you can relax, spend time in convivial company or withdraw for a little peace and quiet and enjoy your garden in all its glory, number among the most important features of any garden. Patios and other seating areas, whether fixed or temporary, usually allow you to experience the garden from close to the house, but pergolas, bowers, pavilions and summerhouses have other advantages – they are often designed as retreats, secluded places that allow you to experience the garden from a new perspective.

Although such structures could be called 'rooms', the majority are not totally enclosed, often being open to the sky and sun above, or partly or completely open to the garden from the sides. However, partially closed off with walls, trellises and climbing plants, they provide a protected vantage point from which to contemplate just a small part of the garden, which can take on its own character as a result. Elements like these have a place in every garden, whatever its size or style. If they are near the house, their style, design, materials and colour should be co-ordinated with the house. However, you have scope for making more original designs if you put them out of the way or out of direct sight. They are then free to steal the limelight, meeting your requirements and becoming a feature in themselves. Alternatively, they can, of course, be made to blend into their surroundings, hiding beneath a green mantle and being transformed into true hideaways. Summerhouses and pavilions are

Traditional design. The intersection of several narrow paths lined with low box hedges is marked by this classical, octagonal wooden arbour, painted pure white. The high roof is interwoven with leafy green, while the diamond-shaped wall panelling provides a decorative touch.

perfect for emphasizing the structure of formal gardens. In small gardens, pergolas can form a stylistic contrast with the house itself, while the presence of a bower in a wild, romantic garden is virtually essential.

Heavenly impressions and shadow games

Pergolas, and their relatives, bowers and leafy walkways, are the airiest of all the garden structures. At their simplest, they have supporting posts and rounded or squared cross-beams. They invariably have an open roof; when unplanted, this allows you to gaze freely up into the changing vista of the sky, but they are usually clad with vines and other climbers, creating cool shade beneath. Pergolas originated in southern countries where they provided a blissful relief in the often stifling heat. But even in a temperate climate we appreciate the shade they offer on hot sunny days, as well as the fascinating play of light and shade that takes place beneath them. Other plus points are the seclusion they offer and the opportunity to display attractive climbing plants.

More down to earth

In contrast to the pergola, pavilions and summerhouses provide a roof over our heads, giving us a real refuge during intemperate weather. If their walls are open, they can be filled with trelliswork, which can then even be glazed for a cosier effect, affording greater protection from the elements.

Above: *Dizzy heights. All children dream of having their very own tree house. The feeling of freedom among the treetops, high above the ground, simply cannot be bettered. If the house is actually built in a tree, the tree must be large and stable enough to bear its weight. Otherwise, wooden stilts, as here, make a very good alternative.*

Below: *A seat by the water's edge has its own particular charm. Reached only by means of a narrow path over the water, this is a truly tranquil retreat.*

Above: *Romantic appeal. This romantic log cabin-style summer house has almost modern appeal, its charm owing much to the alternating birch poles used in the design. The bright white window shutters provide a delightful contrast.*

Below: *Light elegance. This scene is reminiscent of a romantic painting of a country garden. The pavilion is both an attractive seat in the midst of the greenery and an important design feature. The restrained, neat, almost plain design contrasts with the lushness and exuberance of the surrounding vegetation.*

Constructing Frames for Climbing Plants

Page 54, top left: *The identical, rhythmic positioning of wooden trellised archways creates depth and perspective. The gable-like design gives the faint impression of one long but very transparent building that is almost church-like in effect.*

Page 54, top right: *Trelliswork archways are important design elements in gardens, providing height and emphasizing entrances, and they invite you to walk under them to enjoy their glorious sweet-smelling roses, clematis and so on.*

Page 54, bottom left: *Where single arches are linked to form a leafy walkway, the effect is considerably more natural and intimate when climbers are planted at their base. A canopy of climbing plants creates a pleasantly cool and shady atmosphere.*

Page 54, bottom right: *This variation on the trellised arch, constructed from strangely shaped unstripped branches, is not for everyone, but will certainly catch the eye.*

Privacy is maintained elegantly and effectively here with these half-transparent wooden trelliswork walls. A bower seat provides the finishing touch.

Top: *Fence and bench here form a unified whole. Identical materials, styles and colours generate a harmonious, yet by no means monotonous scene.*

Right-hand page: *This seat's natural charm is augmented by its being located among plants in the shade of a tree.*

Below left: *Wooden benches are often painted in bright colours. However, they lose none of their appeal when left untreated.*

Below right: *Spread throughout the garden, benches help create seating areas that provide different aspects and cater for every mood.*

Choosing Useful and Decorative Garden Furniture

A garden should always be planned using the following general principles. First decide on the general layout and the shape of the various areas, so you can accommodate all the functions, activities and themes you have in mind. Then move on to the positions and appearance of the various structures and the choice of plants and materials. This provides you with a definite framework. All that then remains is for you to embellish your design using furniture, sculpture, decorations and other eyecatching features, and permanent or temporary splashes of colour.

Places to relax and linger

Garden furniture is predominantly functional. Tables, benches, stools, seats and sun-loungers, parasols, screens and awnings make life in the open air more agreeable. At the same time, they have a significant effect on the way the garden looks, so careful choice is essential. Garden furniture must, of course, be comfortable, especially if you are settling in for a long, relaxing stay! A chair that is beautiful to look at but uncomfortable to sit in will soon be put to one side.

It is not surprising that wood is often the first choice for garden furniture. It is warm and pleasant to touch and has a further advantage in that it can be worked into a huge variety of forms and shapes and can therefore be adapted to every style and taste. If you choose a weatherproof wood such as teak or kambala, you will not need to give it a protective coat of

These colourful little wooden houses provide shelter and nesting sites for birds. Cats can be deterred by winding thorns or something similar around the supporting post. Take care when using garden features like these – the decorative aspect can easily take over at the expense of the function.

varnish. And it can stay outside the whole year round, weathering accordingly.

If you find this an unattractive idea, you can use oils to maintain the wood's natural tone, or choose a paint or stain in a different colour to make it stand out.

Consider the style of your house and your garden before you buy, then choose something that has a pleasing design and co-ordinates or contrasts with them, this will ensure that it will not be too garish or seem out of place. Good-quality garden furniture is a lasting investment. The cheapest solutions are not always the best, so don't choose something for its price alone.

Setting the tone

A beautiful garden is a pleasure in its own right. Nevertheless, a certain amount of decoration is often desirable, and can add to the effect of the garden as a whole. Pretty little artefacts in just the right place can make secluded areas catch the eye, enhancing the atmosphere and mood of the garden, and by regularly changing them you will be able to constantly create new and interesting impressions. In the past, ornamentation was an integral part of garden design, and included embellishments such as sculptures, symbols, figurines and vases.

Today, the choice is even more varied and entirely up to you, the only guideline being the style of your garden. Formal gardens gain the requisite classical touch through vases, amphoras, figurines and columns. Modern

Above: Dovecotes are still found in some courtyards and villages. They have often been designed with much love and care, which shows in their highly decorative appearance. Occupied or not, it is definitely worth getting one and looking after it, both as a testimony to days gone by and as a garden feature for the present.

Below: Sunbathing by the pool. Unusual carvings like this figure are quite popular. However, their use should be strictly limited, to stop your garden from becoming too kitsch. Yet as an amusing one-off feature, why not?

sculptures can be wonderful, whether on their own or placed among plants. However, you should never forget the cardinal rule, whatever the style and decoration of the garden: ornamentation is only the finishing touch, the icing on the cake, and should be used sparingly. In other words, our attention should, on the whole, be drawn to the garden itself.

Handy hint
Never forget that decor is merely a garden accessory. If you do decide to decorate more extensively, use a consistent style to avoid spoiling the overall atmosphere of the garden.

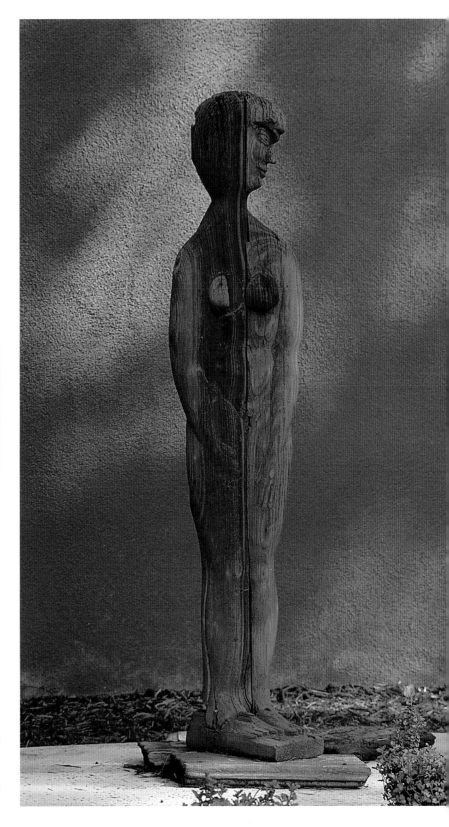

Art in the open air. Sculptures such as this example in wood are perfectly suited to gardens. Here, the intensely red wall acts as a canvas for the play of light and shade, creating a constantly changing backdrop. However, plants, whether green or flowering, are also capable of performing this supporting role and can enhance and intensify the mood and effect.

STONE – NATURAL, DEPENDABLE AND UNCHANGING

Unlock the Potential of Stone

Paths, patios, steps, walls, columns and pillars for fences and pergolas contribute significantly to a garden's overall appearance. It is only commonsense, therefore, that they are planned with the utmost care, using the best possible materials. The oldest, most traditional and most durable of these materials is stone. Its timeless beauty is unaffected by its place in the design, whether in the foreground (see pages 62–64) or dominated by the green of the lawn (right).

Why Stone?

Stone is associated with durability, timelessness, top quality – often with a high price tag – and a rustic or elegant appearance depending on what type it is and how it is processed – think of the difference between York stone and polished marble. Stone should never be expected to take a back seat in proceedings: it is far too good for that! It always catches the eye and, although often subtle, is rarely unobtrusive, which is just as it should be: it can only be obtained with a lot of effort and technical skill and it is a finite resource, a fact that makes it invaluable. When you decide to use it in your garden, plan very carefully and make sure that you, and others after you, will love what you have created, bearing in mind that any structures built from stone will last for decades.

To radiate the peace and stillness that is unique to it, stone must be in the correct environment and it must be used sympathetically. Great craftsmanship, all the knowledge and skill of the stonemason, is required to do stone justice. A good stonemason is able to appreciate and recognize the characteristic features of each piece, and then combine them to form a pleasing and technically perfect construction. There is a reason why we refer to the *art* of stonemasonry. All things considered, we should not think of stone as too expensive. It is not expensive as such, but instead valuable in the best sense, worth every penny, just like the stonemason's expertise.

Upon first consideration, stone may seem a cold inert material. However, its individual grain, colouring, structure and texture can mean it radiates a sense of warmth and comfort. Stone is, in itself, cold, but it is excellent at retaining heat. Walls, flagstones and paving stones heated by the sun's rays stay warm for many hours, long after the sun has set. This is something to bear in mind when creating seats

Left-hand page: *Stone as a central theme. Cream-coloured stone is the main design material in this garden. It positively gleams in the sunlight.*

Right: *Unity of plants and stone. Here, the ivy complements the stone wall, which blends seamlessly with the water trough below, fitting in perfectly with the calming green of the plants – in all a very tranquil scene.*

for warm evenings! But the coolness of stone is also one of its big advantages, especially on a day of scorching sun – then a cool shady wall becomes a real treat.

Types of rock

Natural stone comes in countless different types and colours and has many origins and characteristics; the many different methods of processing can provide further variety in each type of stone. Such processing and presentation makes stone even better to look at and touch. It is truly a very versatile material.

Stone can be divided into three major groups. **Solidified rock or magma** is the solidified product of molten silicates from the centre of the earth. It is possible to differentiate between rocks which have slowly solidified in the earth's interior (plutonic or igneous rock) and those types that have hardened more quickly while breaking through the earth's crust and emerging (volcanic or seamed rock). Granite is a type of plutonic rock, while basalt, lava, tuff and pumice belong to the volcanic group.

Deposited or sedimentary rock is produced over a long period of time when rocks and other substances are eroded by wind, water or ice, carried off and subsequently deposited. This group includes sandstone, gompholite, greywacke, travertine, Jura limestone and muschelkalk.

Finally, the group classified as **transforming rock or metamorphic rock** includes magma, sedimentary rock and older types of metamorphic rock, whose formation or density have been changed as a result of great pressure or exposure to high temperatures. Examples of this process of change include lime (which turns to marble), coal (which turns to slate) and granite (which becomes gneiss).

A further basic method of classifying stone, of particular interest to the gardener, is the subdivision into hard and soft stone. All types of magma, as well as certain types of metamorphic rock, belong in the **hard stone** category. And they are distinguished by their strength and weather-resistant qualities. Granite, syenite, diabas, gabbro, gneiss, basalt, basalt lava, porphyry and volcanic tuff belong in this category.

The **soft stone** category encompasses the sedimentary rocks, stratiform rocks and the vast majority of metamorphic rocks including, for example, sandstone, quartz, greywacke, gompholite, lime, limestone slabs, muschelkalk, travertine and tuff. The rocks in this second group have different levels of toughness and durability, and you must allow for these inherent characteristics when deciding which one to use. Limestone slabs, for example, are not suitable for use in the open air, although small pieces work nicely in protected areas.

Origins

As with everything else, your taste will determine to a great extend the type of stone you choose for your garden. Other considerations are the style of your house and, of course, your budget, as well as what you want to build. Many people decide against importing stone from other countries because it is not very environmentally-friendly to do this, usually takes a lot of time for the stone to get to you and is generally expensive in comparison with local stone. The best solution is to stay closer to home and use native stone. The other really key advantage of using local stone is that it will immediately fit in with your environment. This means that some of your design work is done for you. However, if you want to make a strong statement in your garden, local stone is unlikely to be your choice.

A feeling of weightlessness. This stone plateau seems to hover over the water's surface, denying its own weight and density. The effect of this precisely finished stone is not oppressive, due, in part, to the patterns of the shadows and the green surroundings.

Paths, Steps and Surfaces – Endless Variations

Left: *Putting strong horizontal lines along the course of a long, narrow path is a simple but highly effective way to make it look shorter and wider. Here, solid slabs, interspersed with plants and other materials, create a pleasing effect and hold our interest.*

Above: *Paving slabs are framed by different ornamental grasses, the two blending together because of the use of soft natural tones, from beige and light grey to warmer shades of brown. And yet a contrast is also created between the solid, static path and the tall grasses waving in the wind.*

Opening Up the Garden

Starting off

Think of paths, patios, seats, steps and stairs as essential garden props – man-made structures linking the house with nature. They are part of the garden's enduring features, a presence in all weathers and throughout the seasons. Their worth is particularly appreciated during the winter months, when few plants are in flower and many have died down underground. Of course, winter is also a time when any weak points and blemishes will be fully visible, as there is nothing to hide behind.

Before you start, carefully consider all the surfaces and structures you intend to create in the garden. Their actual design depends significantly on the effect you want to achieve.

Left: Oriental flair. Grey pebbles and gravel in different shades combine here to create a variable and attractive surface.

Below: Country charm. This scene is reminiscent of a cottage garden. A double row of bricks serves as a pretty but practical border, separating path and flowerbed. Unity is provided by the use of gravel and bricks of the same colour.

Right: *This is a surface you are more likely to simply admire than walk on! The clay pots continue the colour scheme of the red paving strips, while the glass fragments are brought to life by the rays of the sun.*

Below: *Although formally designed, this little garden looks far from staid and static, thanks to the soft texturing produced by the use of gravel and bark chippings and the plants in the centre spilling out over their borders.*

Straight designs, lines and angles suit formal gardens and modern minimalist creations. Rounded, wavy, soft and other loose forms are better in more natural gardens and for abstract designs. Although it is possible to combine free and formal designs, this does require great skill. While you can experiment to a certain extent in a large area, careful planning is absolutely essential in smaller gardens. In a limited space, everything is immediately in view, and mistakes are mercilessly exposed. In such situations it is far better to stick consistently to a single theme. To have style you need to be decisive. While you might wish that you could include all the elements you admire, it is far better to stick to just one or two.

Above: *Paths open up the garden, linking its different areas. In many cases, a lovingly laid, narrow, little path, like this one, will do very nicely.*

Below: *Here, scale and form are in harmony. Large stone slabs give the patio an air of spaciousness.*

Practical requirements

The width of a path generally depends on its importance to the user. Main pathways, the backbone of the garden, or those leading to the entrance of the house, should allow enough room for two people to walk comfortably side by side – a width of 1.2m (4ft) should suffice. Paths that are not so frequently used, can be narrower – a width of 30cm (1ft) is enough for little walkways leading to secluded corners of the garden – while paths that double as driveways must be at least 2.5–3m (8–10ft). The surface of a path is directly related to its intended use. Paths used continually the whole year round must be stable, and a non-slip surface is essential. 'Summer' paths, and narrow tracks leading to more remote areas of the garden, will be perfectly acceptable made with grass, bark, gravel or stone chippings.

To ensure paths stay attractive and are good to walk on all year long, they require a firm, stable foundation; this will stop them subsiding and becoming hazardous as well as unattractive. Before you lay the path put in a weight-bearing layer of compressed gravel or hardcore for this crucial supporting role. You may also need to make the path frost-proof, depending on your local conditions.

In addition, you will need to consider the matter of drainage – a must for any type of path, patio or driveway. You can allow for drainage by making sure there is a reasonable slope off the surface. A gradient of 1.5–2 per cent is usually sufficient if you are using smooth,

completely flat materials. It is the ideal for an area that is going to be used for seating and a table, where you want things to be as level as possible. Where the surface material is quite uneven, the gradient must be 3–4 per cent to allow the water to drain off fully. If the area is away from the house, so you cannot use the house's drainage system, you will need to put in a soakaway or ditch to remove any excess water.

Patterns

Although paths, patios and driveways have practical uses, they are also decorative features. Their materials, styles and patterns, and the way they are laid out, all contribute to the garden's overall character. Small areas and narrow paths can look very effective when they are made with smaller patterned paviors or pieces of stone, while larger areas are better covered with bigger slabs, and can be made to appear even more spacious through the use of large flat slabs or paving stones.

Edges

If the surface is a driveway or a similar area that is very heavily used, it is essential to allow for

Handy hint
Decorative paving and attractive plant displays should never compete with one another. So you must decide at the planning stage where the emphasis should be and which of these two will set the tone.

A successful mix of materials and colour. Shiny red tiles and bright natural stone paving divide up this generous patio in a strictly geometric theme.

supportive and protective edging. This can, for example, take the form of edging stones or kerbing, which should then be secured in place with concrete.

With paths that take only foot traffic, edging is optional and is usually included purely for its stylistic effect. Edging of this kind is flexible and can become a decorative feature in itself; it can be deliberately separated from the path with gravel or plants, or it can follow it exactly; it can be wide and obvious (right), it can boldly point the way forward, taking the form a grand gesture, such as the wall above, or it can be narrow and fairly inconspicuous.

Handy hint
Stepping stones, either laid directly on the lawn (see above) or in the midst of a lush planting of perennials, are perfect for paths that are not in constant use and do not require a particularly strong base. They are easy to lay and very pleasing to the eye.

Surface texture

The most natural stone surface is one that is roughly broken or cracked. All types of stone look wonderful like this, as it reveals their true character and texture. This sort of surface is ideal for paths as it is less likely to be slippery when wet or covered with algae.

Although common indoors, sanded and polished surfaces are rarely used outdoors: they are too dangerous when wet. While you can get away with using marginally smoother stones on a patio, you should bear in mind that they might become slippery, particularly if the patio is in the shade or badly drained. For example, slate tends to have a smooth surface that attracts algae. You could score it to make more non-slip, but this seems a pity as it is so beautiful. Nowadays, concrete paving is made to look like stone. It tends to have a rougher or imitation riven surface and is ideal for patios and paths.

Right: *Enclosed on both sides. Bright limestone has been used to make the risers on these steps, and the gravel surface on the treads perfectly matches its colour.*

Below: *An effective use of small parts. Small pieces of limestone laid diagonally are used to great effect in the construction of this superb stepped path, achieving an engaging mosaic feel.*

Chessboard pattern. In this boldly designed patio, rectangular slabs and strips of grass are interwoven into an interesting pattern of light and dark. Any more colour would be superfluous.

Filling in the gaps

If conventional surfaces are too austere or monotonous for your taste, they can be spiced up by introducing greenery into gaps in the paving. There are many ways of doing this, but the classic method is to sow grass between the flags. You simply lay the stones with gaps of, say, 2–5cm (about 1–2in) in between, then fill the resulting spaces with a mixture of chippings, to ensure the necessary cohesion, and humus to ensure proper plant growth, and grass seed. It is advisable to use special grass-seed mixtures that are recommended by their producers for growing in dry places – some might even say that they are ideal for planting between paving on the packet. Growing conditions in between the paving stones are far from ideal for most grasses, so it really isn't worth splashing out on a luxury grass-seed mixture of the sort intended for a lawn.

Another extremely effective and popular choice for patio and seating areas is to add low-growing plants to the gaps in between the paving slabs. There are many plants (see Handy hint for some) that relish the conditions and will spring up all over the place to add spots of colour and scent just where you can most appreciate it. You can allow them to spread naturally and just remove those that are not in the right place, or you can plant them in a pattern to produce a more formal result. Alternatively, for a much bolder effect, make larger spaces, perhaps the size of a paving stone, in just a few places around the patio and plant a few bigger plants in them.

Page 82 left: Colonies of violets seem so at home on this patio, forming a lively contrast with the tranquil, subdued surface. Islands of plants such as these needn't prevent you from using the patio in the normal way.

Page 82 right: The art of combining. A soft cushion of lawn pearlwort (Sagina subulata) thrives between the square slabs. Throughout summer decorative white flowers hover over the needle-like foliage which remains attractive for the whole year.

Handy hint
The herbaceous perennials suitable for open paving include lawn pearlwort, chamomile and various dwarf varieties of thyme and mint. They create pretty carpets, and the chamomile, thyme and mint also release delightful aromas when walked upon.

A special form of pondside planting. Brilliant light yellow sedum flowers are delightfully combined with light green granite, creating a singular composition.

Inspired Combinations

Left: *Simple, yet decorative. No corner of the garden should be neglected. Even the area where you put the rubbish bins can be well designed as shown here.*

Below: *A radial layout around a perfectly round centre stone with gravel filling the spaces in between gives this appealing composition a sense of movement.*

Right: *A mixture of materials and shapes. Wooden blocks alternated with pebbles make an attractive path. However, a similar but safer solution would be to use stone with a rough surface instead of wood. It will then be less slippery to walk on when it is wet.*

Below: *Treads made from broken stone lead you through the gravel surface like stepping stones in water. Unnecessary from a purely functional point of view, they are a crucial element of the design.*

Left: *An unusual contrast of light and dark. Surfaces such as these are not really for walking on; rather the intention is to create an eyecatching patterned carpet..*

Below left: *Magnificent ornamental pebble paths, such as those found in the Mediterranean, are the main influence in this courtyard design. After rain, the smooth stones shine as if they have been polished and the contrast between the colours becomes even more vivid.*

Below right: *This surface comes to life when the evening's warm reddish light makes the grey-brown stones begin to glow. The fragmented stones give the surface extra grip, making it safer to walk on, and the pebbles increase its decorative value.*

Left: *This ornamental feature is made from different-coloured pebbles and emphasizes the tree trunk – making something that might have been overlooked the centre of attention.*

Right: *Although only one type of pebble is used here, this path has a lively pattern. The changes in direction and the variation of the placement of the stones make for an arresting display and are an indicator of the skill and artistry of its builder.*

Walls – Enclosing and Separating Spaces

Left: *Almost the entire wall coping has been taken over by roses, their cream coloured flowers softening its harsh edges. The paving around the pool matches the stones of the wall. The red brick path that divides them is a bold feature.*
Above: *The creator of this garden feature has successfully broken with the conventions of style and proportion. When you see this giant head peering over the parapet, you almost expect the rest of the torso to be lying behind the low rustic wall.*

The Beauty of a Wall

In gardens, walls have various functions to fulfil: they protect against the elements, particularly the wind, and provide privacy; they create separate areas by enclosing or dividing; and they can be used to provide backdrops for seating areas or statues, pots and other artefacts. Last but not least, they are invaluable for overcoming differences in height within a plot when they are built to retain soil and create terracing.

Natural dry stone walls

In wide open areas, walls play an important role; many areas of Britain would change their character completely if the walls were taken away – think of the stone banks of Devon and Cornwall and the walls of the Peaks and Lake District. Although man-made, many are so old that they seem to have grown there, and these areas would look less beautiful without them. Traditional walls are most frequently of a dry stone construction: there is nothing joining the individual stones together, they are simply arranged one beside the other, one on top of the other. If you look at these walls, however, there is nothing rough in their make up – the stones are often laid as neatly as bricks, each chosen to fit precisely with its neighbour. This gives them a unique strength that means they can last for decades without damage. In some cases they are so strong that they can support the weight and roots of trees without buckling. Dry stone walls have a character that is unique. They seem to exude life, and indeed they do provide a home for plants and animals. In the countryside, ferns, grasses, bluebells, primroses and many other plants, as well as birds and small rodents, thrive under their protection.

Making a choice

Natural stone is the material of choice for building walls. Its appeal is not just its durability

Below left: Walls made from boulders that have had little or no man-made processing give this garden a particularly rustic character.

Below right: A dry stone wall provides a natural home for plants that thrive in open gaps and flowers that enjoy living on the top of a wall.

and adaptability but also its appearance – its range of colours and textures, and the fact that it so suits its environment. However, natural stone can be extremely expensive and most of us have to make do with cheaper options. You might be lucky enough to have a quarry near you, which makes things a lot cheaper, but unless you have plenty of money, you are likely to have to opt for some of the more attractive stone reproductions that are made out of concrete. Over recent years, manufacturers of these products have put a lot of effort into

making them look more realistic, and, as a result, there is quite a wide choice available. There is still some way to go before they look like real stone, but the more you can afford to spend, the more attractive the product. If you can afford natural stone, it is best to use that which is indigenous to your area, or to limit non-local stone to small features. For example, honey-coloured Cotswold stone looks out of place in a grey granite area and although you could still use it, it would never blend in with the surroundings.

Dry stone walls radiate a sense of liveliness with their surface textures and the changes from light to shadow within their joints. Despite its show of strength, stone can be used in large quantities without being overpowering.

The Beauty of a Wall   91

Stone – a Perfect Partner

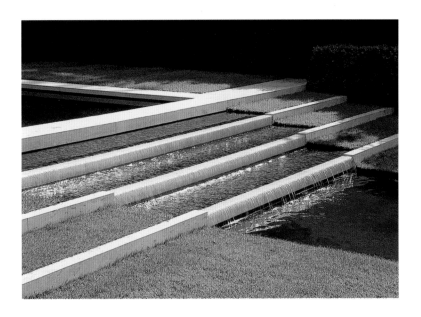

Left: *Just like a natural spring, this man-made stream playfully splashes down around the boulders, flowing from stone to stone.* Above: *Here, grass steps merge seamlessly with water steps almost seeming to become part of them. The horizontal lines of the pale-coloured stone unify the design providing a strong contrast to both the grass and the water.*

Stone and Water

Water and stone are often used together in gardens. These two elements could not be more different, yet they become the perfect partners in a well-designed water feature. Water can be flowing and volatile, constantly changing its appearance, gurgling and splashing, foaming and glistening as the rays of the sun sparkle on its surface. It can also be calm, smooth and reflective when there is no wind or movement to disturb its smooth surface or its dark and impenetrable depths. In contrast, stone is completely static; it is so solid-looking

Left: In natural water features, barriers are best made of simple broken stones. In just a short while, the dampness will encourage moss and algae to grow, giving the impression that this miniature dam has always been there.

Below, left: Here, the water and the accompanying plants are the principal features. But the loosely arranged stones that follow the course of the stream provide an important additional focus.

Below, right: This fountain was made from solid, natural stone and makes an attractive focal point. The pebbles around its base contribute to the effect.

Right-hand page: There is something about stepping stones that brings us closer to the liveliness of water. Here they have been put across an area of still water and the straight line they create enhances the overall tranquility of the scene.

and durable, never changing, whatever the weather or the season. Perhaps this is why water and stone make ideal partners, each enhancing the effect of the other, precisely because of these obvious contrasts, and together creating something totally new.

A heavenly match?

Think about a stone fountain without water. No matter how attractive the design of the fountain, unless it has water running through it, it lacks life and interest, and seems pointless. But once someone turns on the tap, the two elements are like a magnetic force, becoming one of the main highlights in any garden, contributing immeasurably to the pleasure of time spent outdoors and providing a place of tranquility and relaxation and a source of sensory stimulation. The atmosphere created by water in any form is always special. And stone can really liven up the mood. It doesn't matter whether it is the water or the stone that plays the dominant role.

Unlike a stone wall, a stone water feature is much more affordable for everyone because you can limit the amount you use. Just one large bolder can look good, while several as a series of stepping stones across a little stream will go a long way to creating just the right kind of riverside atmosphere. A couple of roughly broken stones or hewn blocks are ideal for 'water breakers' in brooks and ponds and can have just as pleasing an effect as a fountain crafted by a stonemason or a sculptor.

Stone and Garden Buildings

From a design point of view, garden structures, such as summerhouses, pergolas and gazebos, have a variety of functions. They can act as purely decorative pieces, highlights, islands of calm amid the seasonally changing nature of the vegetation, and counterpoints to the house. They are also simple yet delightful places to allow you to pause in the middle of the garden, somewhere you to are close to nature but also have a feeling of protection and security. If you are overlooked, they allow you to enjoy the garden without being seen by the neighbours. Structures that have roofs and walls offer shelter from the elements, too.

The design of these buildings should reflect or complement the design of the garden and must not clash with the house. Because of planning

Top: *This striking garden building is part treehouse and part summerhouse. Perhaps the owner wanted to fulfil a childhood dream, or maybe just get a different perspective of the garden.*

Below: *Pavilions work especially well with formal gardens that follow a historical model or in romantic and dreamy surroundings. Brick is a good alternative to natural stone.*

regulations, most of us have to make do with wooden structures, however, if you can get permission to build a more permanent structure, natural stone is among the best material to use. It is so versatile, and whether rough-hewn or finely finished always produces spectacular results. For inspiration, visit some of the historical gardens around the country where designers such as Gertrude Jekyll and Lancelot 'Capability' Brown constructed fine pergolas, follies, summerhouses and orangeries,

that make their mark on the garden but also often blend into the landscape, too. Of course, you are unlikely to be able to reproduce their designs exactly but it will give you an idea of the type of thing that is possible, with a little effort. Alternatively, consider the work of some modern landscape designers, such as John Brookes, Diarmuid Gavin, Bonita Bulaitis and Dan Pearson. Their ideas are often readily adaptable and can work wonderfully well in the right setting.

This pergola has been built in a modern style, but is based on traditional forms. Brilliant white polished columns support the transparent roof, making a cool, elegant composition.

Above left: *Stone guards. Sentinel-like, four pillars gather at the edge of the pond, silently observing the tranquil scene.*

Above right: *Creating a window. This moongate is constructed entirely without mortar, each stone supports the next. It is a fine example of the craftsmanship of its creator.*

Bottom: *Side by side. Cacti and pebbles sit snugly together in a miniature meditation garden. A new take on the potted plant.*

Top: *Secret view. The eyes of this garlanded head seem to follow the visitor round the garden. Reliefs like these are ideal for wall fountains.*

Centre: *Layered work. Hundreds of plate-like stones have been arranged by hand to make this wonderful vase. The result is a true work of art and a perfect example of the possibilities of dry stone constructions.*

Bottom: *Imperishable fruits. Ornaments like these become more attractive with time as they are gradually covered by moss and lichen.*

BRICKS AND TILES –
TRADITIONAL,
TIMELESS AND VERSATILE

From Clay to Brick

Only a few building materials have the ability to look just right, while fulfilling many design criteria, both in the home and in the garden. But one that demonstrates such versatility is the brick and its immediate relatives, other clay-based products. In bricks, clay and loam are refined into a material that is undeniably artificial and yet fits perfectly with natural surroundings, can make a bold statement or retires into the background. Bricks are available in many colours and finishes, as the photographs on 100–101 reveal, and they can be laid in many different patterns (left).
Right: Simple terracotta tiles, a close relation to the brick, are laid slightly irregularly and with some suitable props to evoke a Mediterranean feel.

Materials with Many Possibilities

Bricks are a very simple product. They contain clay and loam and there are various mixtures of clay with other aggregates, such as sand or ashes. They come in a wide variety of colours, including warm tones of yellow or ochre to various red and brown shades, it is even possible to find them in blue-black and dark anthracite. The colour depends on the type of clay used, the minerals that it contains and the firing process. Pure colours are just as feasible as shades. To ensure that the colours will not fade with time, the raw materials have to be free from impurities and of the same consistency and colouring throughout.

The production of bricks is straightforward. The ingredients are mixed together and then moulded into a brick shape; they are then dried and fired at very high temperatures of between 800 and 1200° C (1472 to 2192° F) for about three days. Clinkers differ from bricks in that they are fired at a higher temperature until they become pore-free and extremely tough, which makes them frost-resistant and extremely hard-wearing. Imitation bricks, made from pressed concrete, are also widely available and come in a wide variety of designs and colours.

Top left: Feather in his cap. This slightly comic clay head sits among plants and wears an ironic smile.

Top right: Clay on clay contrast. Bricks and terracotta: two completely different products with the same origins. This scene is harmonious at the same time as being quite striking.

Left: A cute piglet stands guard by the front door; a good luck charm.

Top left: *As if by chance. A group of spheres of varying size and texture, and made from different coloured clays, make up this novel feature.*

Top right: *Light design in blue. A voluptuous and curvy woman, made completely out of blue mosaic tiles and reflective mirrors, sparkles in the sun. Ornaments such as this one add to a garden's appeal.*

Below: *Peace and tranquillity. Ferns and other shade-lovers have colonized this bench. It is made from old bricks, and their weathered appearance gives the impression that they have always been here.*

Paths, Steps and Walls – Showy or Subtle

Left: *Herringbone is a traditional brick-laying pattern. Here the designer has cleverly linked the house with the patio by using the same red bricks. Had the patio been attached to the house, this colour-matching might have been too much, as it is, it simply ensures an understated unity.*

Above: *Although subtly set off by the flowers, the strongest colour here, a cool red, is provided by the bricks. The grey shades of the concrete, the chippings and the natural stone wall make them all pleasing partners.*

Choosing and Using Bricks

Bricks have various advantages when it comes to paths and outdoor seating areas. They are relatively non-slip and can be used to make a wide variety of shapes and patterns. They are also long-lasting with an enduring and increasing beauty. If you are planning to use them in shady areas, bear in mind that they can still get slippery as they seem to attract moss – part of their charm. Smoother bricks are more likely to become slippery than the rougher types. One of the reasons bricks can be used in so many ways is the fact they are available in a range of shapes. The most popular is the traditional 'brick' with its regular dimensions – about 214 × 100 × 60mm (8^1/$_2$ × 4 × 2^1/$_2$in). The relationship between these dimensions allows them to be used in a variety of ways – for example, the length is twice the width with a little extra for the mortar, allowing for neat and attractive bonding (the way the bricks overlap in a wall). If you want to use straightforward building bricks in your garden, make sure you choose the correct type. The cheaper varieties, which are fine for walls, will not stand up to the

Above left: An elegant touch. This brown-black wall provides the ideal backdrop for the floral ornament, which is made from black iron.

Above right: The interplay of light and dark. The solid brick walls and filigree iron furniture are enlivened by the rich floral upholstery.

sort of conditions that they will experience when laid on a patio or path – frost, frequent or constant wet on all sides and heavy use. They will not weather nicely (as they would on a wall) but, instead, simply crumble.

While the traditional clay brick is excellent for the garden, it is also worth considering the various pressed-concrete varieties that are widely available. These may lack some of the 'naturalness' of brick, but they are very versatile and are particularly suitable for areas that receive a great deal of use, such as driveways.

These products often also have matching items that can be incorporated into a design, kerbs for example. It is even possible to get curved 'bricks', so you can make a very neat circle or a series of wavy shapes. These are particularly useful for breaking up larger areas.

Simulated granite setts are another interesting product, widely used in shopping centres and towns. In the right environment and used sparingly, however, they can look very realistic and they are much easier to lay than the real thing – and cheaper.

Pages 108/109 centre: *Brought into line. Bricks are used here to good effect on the patio and steps.*

Above left: *A novel feature. The brick moongate delightfully frames a garden scene beyond.*

Top right: *Sweeping entrance. The curve of the steps makes them look shorter and less steep inviting you to go up.*

Making Patterns

The character of a brick surface is largely decided by the laying pattern. With rectangular bricks there are various patterns, or bonds, that can be used, alone or in combination. Probably the most common pattern for frequently-used surfaces is herringbone (p.106). For pathways, patios and seating areas, there is also stretcher bond (p.111, bottom right), which is how one thinks of walls being built – bricks in parallel rows but each row evenly staggered, so that the joints of alternate rows line up. In English cross bond, alternating rows of bricks are set lengthways and crossways, with the joints of the alternate rows lining up. Flemish bond is similar except that the bricks are laid lengthways and crossways within each row. With basketweave (p111, top left), pairs of bricks are laid at right angles to each other. Combinations of patterns can be used to define different areas. Before you choose, experiment to see how a pattern looks over the area to be covered.

Top: The muted, relatively dark, colouring of this patio contributes to the overall restful feeling of the delightful, shady seating area.

Above: This lively chessboard layout has been produced by combining brown to blue-black bricks and light-coloured pebbles. The variations in materials and colours has ensured the area, which is quite large, doesn't look empty.

Top left: *'Stepping stones' made from light red bricks that positively invite us to walk on them.*

Top right: *This flaming red patio should give its owners a holiday feeling every day, even though they are in the heart of the city.*

Bottom left: *A truly stunning construction: this luxurious 'carpet' shows just what can be achieved using a variety of bricks.*

Bottom right: *An unusual effect is created here by these brick rugs, which seem almost to have been inserted into the soft green lawn.*

Making Patterns

Tiles and Mosaics

In addition to the 'natural' earthy of bricks, fired clay can be made into extremely attractive colourful tiles. Glazes can be used to make ceramic or stoneware tiles almost any colour, and they then have the potential to create striking eyecatching features. The colour and brilliance of the end product depends on the composition of the glaze and of the tile itself. When choosing tiles, remember that shiny finishes are more conspicuous than matt ones; in well-lit areas, the latter are less obtrusive. If you would like to venture into using terracota tiles, remember that beautiful those they are, they are also usually porous and will crumble with repeated exposure to water. You can counteract this to a certain extent by making a

Left: *The art of mosaic making has a tradition that stretches back thousands of years. Originally clay pieces, pebbles, coloured stones and glass were put together with masterful skill; nowadays we often use broken tiles, which can be very effective.*

Below: *Tracks of deep blue mosaic trickle and meander towards the inner pool, like a series of watercourses. The effect is compounded by the mosaic on the pool walls.*

Right: *Wall murals made from decorative tiles can be used to provide permanent focal points. Particularly artistic examples, such as this one, can be seen in Spain and, especially, Portugal, where magnificent hand-painted 'azulejos', as they are called, adorn the inside and outside of almost every house.*

Below: *Not to everyone's taste, there is no denying that this combination of powerful colours and textures has a strong and immediate impact.*

rigid base out of concrete and using continuous mortar jointing.

Make sure that the tiles you chose can resist frost and will not become slippery. For a large area, where you need a functional, durable material, natural stone, brick or even high-quality concrete slabs are preferable. No matter what you do, tiles will always be more vulnerable to damage from having things dropped on them and uneven wear.

However, it is well worth considering coloured tiles for the construction of small mosaics on a wall or as elegant inlays in a bigger, tougher surface material. They can make excellent focal points and always lend a stylish, individual touch to surfaces made out of other materials.

METAL – AIRY, COOL AND STRIKING

Aluminium, Iron, Copper and Co.

Of all the types of material that are used outdoors, metal is the coolest and feels the least natural, due to the extensive processing it usually undergoes to acquire its final form. Modern designs are very different to the traditional ones, but the popularity of both is assured. Metal is so versatile; it can be made into almost any shape or form we desire. Thin sections of iron create a feeling of airiness (pages 114–115), 'waves' made out of sheets of high-quality steel look spectacular and futuristic (left-hand page) and, in the right context, rust (right) can be impressive.

Room for Design

Metal has a clear advantage over stone, wood and clay because of the many different ways it can be manipulated. It can be transformed into practically any shape: whether cast, cut, rolled, joined, riveted, reinforced, pressed or forged — almost anything is possible.

Iron and steel are the most popular materials for using outdoors. Steel is strong and malleable, whereas iron, though strong, is more brittle. Stainless steel will retain its bright shine, but otherwise both have a tendency to rust, which can be attractive in the appropriate setting. Aluminium and copper, and their alloys, brass and bronze, are also very easy to shape into various forms. They are resistant to corrosion. Verdigris, a beautiful blue-green patina, will slowly form on copper, brass and bronze.

Left: *Tollgate. A unique and unusual archway spans a narrow garden path. Perhaps the striking pose of the iron guard is intended to slow you down, so that you stop for a while and take in the surroundings.*

Top: *Purely for decoration.*
Garden furniture made from
cast iron has a very long
tradition. Its value lies in its
elegance and the fact that it
seems somehow weightless.
Unfortunately, not always
the most comfortable of
seats, but definitely one of
the most decorative.

Below left: *Reflections.*
Modern gardens are rarely
without artefacts made of
high-quality steel, which is
valued for its cool, shiny, sheer
surface. The simpler and more
linear the shapes, the better
the effect.

Below right: *A modern*
coating. Steel is ideal for
making fences and gates. In
this contemporary design,
bands of corten steel (a
weather-resistant steel whose
rust coating is not a sign of
deterioration but rather a
protective layer) are crafted
into an abstract lattice gate.

Page 120: *This undulating*
object made of rusted corten
steel is a sensational work of
art. Its wavy snake-like body
slithers between the hedges,
making a bizarre contrast to
their linear lines.

PRACTICAL SECTION

Plant Lists

Although paths, pergolas, walls and patios, as well as other structures, play a vital role, a garden only really comes alive when the final ingredient is added – the plants. Once these begin to grow up around arches and pergolas, and spread beside paths or patios, the gardener can begin to see the true result of all that hard work. When they are skilfully chosen and placed in the garden, it is the plants that provide that all important link between man-made constructions, no matter how beautiful, and nature. Plants make an arbour or pergola seem as if it had 'grown' where it stands. They help fences to blend in and they create flowing transitions between patios and paths.

The following pages contain lists of climbing plants that are suitable for growing over pergolas and arches, and so on, as well as a selection of plants that can be used to fill gaps in between paving stones on the patio or along paths. The lists are not exhaustive as this is not part of the remit of this book, but they offer a starting point, to give you the inspiration to find out more.

Technical information

After the plant lists, on pages 129–132, there is a short section devoted to information about building some of the items featured in this book, such as retaining walls, patios and steps. Unless you are good at practical work, it is probably best to employ a professional garden builder, who will know exactly what is required. However, these pages will give you an idea of what is involved in each case, so you can make a rough estimate of the sort of costs you might incur for building materials, the type of preparations that might be required for foundations and so on.

Climbing Plants for Arbours, Pergolas and Arches

The tables below contain lists of climbing plants that are suitable for the structures featured in this book. There are three main types of climber, those, such as roses and wisteria, that generally need to be tied to their supports, those that twine (or creep) around suitable supports but may need some help, such as clematis, and those that climb by means of adventitious aerial roots, such as ivy, which manages its ascent without our help. For the garden structures mentioned above, the first two types are most suitable. They include vines, honeysuckle, and Dutchman's pipe. Self-climbers such as ivy, vines, climbing hydrangeas and trumpet vines are ideal for stone or brick surfaces, wooden walls or any close wooden trellis, but do not cling to metal.

The best sorts of supports have a rough surface as this gives the plants something to get hold of, but you will also need to tie them in regularly especially clematis, which will soon tie itself in knots, and roses, the thorns of which will otherwise threaten to attack any passersby. With a suitable support, twining climbers such as honeysuckle will do the job by themselves, but you might need to provide them with some encouragement initially. With self-clingers, just watch them romp away. Make sure that the support matches the climber and will be able to cope with it in all stages of growth. For example, *Clematis montana* is an extremely vigorous plant and will need a very strong frame to clamber over, while many other clematis are fine, light and delicate plants and will never reach much in the way of height, so don't overface them with a huge structure.

In general, climbing plants require more shade when they are planted and becoming established, but as they get older, they flourish in full sun. The base of the plant, however, should be kept in the shade, especially clematis. Most require or prefer a relatively warm location with some frost protection. They should also not be too exposed to the wind. Climbers generally prefer a humid atmosphere and moist but well drained soil. A soil rich in nutrients and humus and slightly acid to neutral is ideal; it should also have a loose texture to allow free drainage – like most other plants, climbers do not like compacted soil.

Botanical name	Common name	Height	Flowers	Situation	Notes
Actinidia arguta	Tara vine	6–8m (20–26ft)	Late spring to early summer Clusters of three, white, fragrant	Sunny to partially shady	Strongly growing creeper; brilliant yellow autumn colouring, gooseberry-like fruits with a high vitamin C content; but in order to obtain fruits, male and female specimens have to be planted together.
Actinidia chinensis	Chinese gooseberry Kiwi fruit	8–10m (26–33ft)	Early summer Creamy white, yellow	Sunny to partially shady	Extremely strong-growing creeper; bears the famous kiwi fruits; needs a warm, protected location; frost-sensitive.
Actinidia kolomikta		3–4m (10–13ft)	Early summer White, fragrant	Sunny to partially shady	Creeper with medium growth for warm and protected locations; extraordinarily decorative, tri-coloured foliage in green, white and pink, colour increases with age; male plants have more interesting colouring, but female plants produce yellow-green fruit.
Akebia quinata	Chocolate vine	6–8m (20–26ft)	Late spring Flowers female: brownish purple, spicily fragrant	Sunny to partially shady	Semi-evergreen creeper with rounded leaves; grows well in mild climates; can be invasive; produces edible fruits about 10cm (4in) long.

Botanical name	Common name	Height	Flowers	Location	Notes
Aristolochia macrophylla	Dutchman's pipe	8–10m (26–33ft)	Early to mid-spring Solitary, round, mid-green	Partially shady to shady	Strong-growing creeper; for north west and east aspects; also succeeds on a south-facing structure; decorative, heart-shaped foliage, overlaps like roof tiles; individual leaves up to 30cm (12in) diameter; fruits are poisonous but seldom appear.
Celastrus orbiculatus	Oriental bittersweet Staff vine	12–14m (40–46ft)	Early summer Green-yellow, unassuming	Sunny to partially shady	Strong-growing creeper with interesting bead-like yellow fruits, that open to reveal pink to red seeds which decorate the garden in winter; very frost-hardy.
Clematis alpina	Alpine clematis	2–3m (6½–10ft)	Late spring to early summer Blue-violet	Slightly shady to shady	Award-winning early-flowering climber; occasionally flowers again in mid- to late summer.
Clematis montana var. rubens		8–10m (26–33ft)	Late spring to early summer Pink, fragrant	Sunny to partially shady, also shady	Strong-growing; good resistance to frost; highly recommended; purple-flushed mid-green foliage.
Clematis tangutica		4–6m (13–20ft)	Midsummer to late autumn Golden-yellow	Sunny to partially shady	Very robust and frost-hardy; abundant bell-shaped flowers are followed by fluffy, silvery seedheads that provide decoration throughout the winter.
Clematis viticella		3–5m (10–16ft)	Summer	Sunny	Of medium growth; nodding flowers on long stems; abundance of flowers over several months; good resistance to frost; very healthy.
Clematis hybrids		2–4m (6½–13ft)	Almost any, depending on the variety	Sunny to partially shady	Extensive range of colours and flower shapes; it is vital to prune at correct time – some flower on previous year's growth.
Humulus lupulus	Hop	2–6m (6½–20ft)	Mid- to late summer Green	Sunny to partially shady	Extremely strong-growing creeper; broadly ovoid, fragrant, green then straw-coloured spikes of female flowers 2cm (¾in) long; award-winning, yellow-leaved variety 'Aureus'.
Lonicera x brownii	Scarlet trumpet honeysuckle	2–3m (6½–10ft)	Summer	Slightly shady to shady	Deciduous or semi-evergreen climber of moderate vigour; sometimes produces red berries.

Climbing Plants for Arbours, Pergolas and Arches

Botanical name	Common name	Height	Flowers	Situation	Notes
Lonicera caprifolium	Italian honeysuckle	4–6 (13–20ft)	Late spring to early summer Yellowish-white, red traces on outside	Sunny to shady	Woody, deciduous, twining climber with grey-green leaves; extremely fragrant 5cm (2in) long flowers are followed by orange-red berries; prune every 2–3 years.
Lonicera x heckrottii		3–4m (10–13ft)	Summer Outside pink, inside orange-yellow	Partially shady	Weak-growing but has unusually attractive flowers; 'Gold Flame' is more vigorous and hardier.
Lonicera henryi		6–8m (20–26ft)	Early to midsummer Yellow-throated, purplish-red	Partially shady to shady	Woody evergreen climber prized for its glossy, dark green foliage; and a strong creeper; one of the few unscented varieties of *Lonicera*; flowers followed by purple-black berries.
Lonicera x tellmanniana		5–6m (16–20ft)	Late spring to early summer Yellow-orange	Sunny to partially shady	Very strong-growing creeper; striking flowers but no scent; attractive foliage, deep green, blue-white beneath.
Rosa	Climbing roses	2–5m (6½–16ft)	Early summer to early autumn All colours and shades of colours	Sunny to partially shady	A group of spreading climbers with a wide variety of flower shapes and colours; as well as the classic single-flowering and perpetual-flowering climbing roses there are the rambling roses, which are particularly good for arbour and pergola greenery with their less vertical habit and their long, extremely flexible stems.
Vitis coignetiae	Vine	6–10m (20–33ft)	Summer Tiny green in panicles	Sunny to partially shady	Strong-growing, woody, deciduous climber; very large coarsely toothed, dark green leaves whose undersides have brown felted hair; magnificent red autumn colouring; bears small unpalatable blue-black grapes.
Vitis vinifera	Domestic grape vine	8–10m (26–33ft)	Summer Green	Sunny to partially shady	Strong-growing climber that attaches itself by tendrils; use only mildew-resistant varieties; annual pruning necessary; useful crops of fruit, even in less favourable, cool climates.
Wisteria floribunda	Japanese wisteria	9–12m (30–40ft)	Early summer Blue to violet, pink or white	Sunny to partially shady	Fully hardy, vigorous, twining climber with pendent racemes of fragrant flowers to 30cm (12in) in length.
Wisteria sinensis	Chinese wisteria	9–12m (30–40ft)	Late spring to early summer Lilac-blue to white	Sunny to partially shady	Hardy, vigorous creeper with pinnate leaves and dense pendent racemes of pea-like flowers often followed by velvety green seedpods; flowers at risk from late frost.

Planting in the Gaps

As well as grass, there is also a large range of herbaceous and evergreen perennials and annuals that can be used to fill the gaps between paving stones and slabs, adding colour and texture. In addition to their decorative leaves and flowers, many of them also enrich the garden with their fragrances or aromas.

The following table mentions a few suitable species, but is by no means exhaustive. A number of the plants featured belong in a rockery or are happy in sunny, dry, exposed areas and have relatively low nutrient requirements. Because they are not fussy or demanding, they are ideally suited to the harsh conditions that are found in between stones. On surfaces that see a lot of use, low-growing species which can cope with being trodden on are ideal. Taller plants can be used to add interest around the edges or in larger island beds. When making your selection, choose robust plants that look attractive over a long period – they will be on full show after all.

In the table, take normal soil to mean not too heavy (clayey) or too light (sandy), nor too acid or too alkaline, and containing a moderate supply of nutrients.

Botanical name	Common name	Height	Flowers	Situation	Notes
Acaena spp.	Bidi-bidi New Zealand burr	5–10cm (2–4in)	Early summer to midsummer Unassuming	Sunny Normal to chalky soil	Evergreen bedding plant with pretty, ornamental foliage; the flowers are inconspicuous but the bristly brown fruit stalks are exceptionally decorative from late summer. A. *microphylla* is particularly striking with small spherical flowerheads followed by bright red burrs.
Alchemilla erythropoda	Lady's mantle	10cm (4in)	Early summer to midsummer Yellowish-green	Sunny Normal, chalky or gravelly	Clump-forming herbaceous perennial with delicate clouds of flowers; honeyed floral scent; this species is lower-growing than A. *mollis* and is not so prolific; can also tolerate shade.
Antennaria spp.	Cat's ears Pussy-toes	10–15cm (4–6in)	Late spring to early summer Pink, white, red	Sunny Sandy soil, not chalky	Mat-forming with silvery-grey carpet of foliage; thrives in extremely dry, sparse, sandy locations; award-winning rose-pink red-flowering variety A. *dioica* 'Rosea'.
Arabis caucasica	Rock cress	15–30cm (6–12in)	Mid- to late spring White	Sunny Normal to chalky soil	Low-maintenance, mat-forming with grey-green foliage and fragrant flowers; many varieties with different-coloured flowers and leaves; short-lived (3–5 years).
Aurinia saxatilis	Gold dust	25–40cm 10–16in)	Mid-spring to late summer Yellow	Sunny Normal soil	Long-lived, low-maintenance cushion herbaceous perennial with lavish, brilliant yellow flowers; pruning required; blooms have a honeyed, flowery scent; roots are sensitive to wet conditions.
Campanula carpatica	Bellflower	20–30cm (8–12in)	Summer Blue, white	Sunny Normal to chalky soil	Stocky cushion-forming herbaceous perennial with fresh green foliage; unfortunately both foliage and roots are popular with slugs and snails!; prized varieties: 'Jewel' and 'Weisse Clips' ('White Clips').

Planting in the Gaps

Botanical name	Common name	Height	Flowers	Situation	Notes
Campanula portenschlagiana	Dalmation bellflower	15cm (6in)	Early to midsummer and early autumn Blue-violet	Sunny to partially shady Normal to chalky soil	Cushion herbaceous perennial with mat- to carpet-like growth; tolerates some shade and dryness; spreads by self-seeding without becoming troublesome; second flowering in autumn if cut back after first flowering.
Cerastium tomentosum var. columnae	Snow-in-summer	10cm (4in)	Late spring to early summer White	Sunny Normal, sandy or loamy soil	Mat or carpet-forming, with attractive silver-grey to white foliage; less invasive than species.
Chamaemelum nobile	Chamomile	20cm (8in)	Summer White	Sunny Light, sandy soil	Herbaceous perennial with filigreed foliage and daisy flowers; leaves and flowers exude an intense fragrance especially when they are walked upon; pretty double-flowering variety 'Flore Pleno'.
Convallaria majalis	Lily of the valley	15–25cm (6–10in)	Late spring to early summer White	Partially shady to shady Damp soil with humus	Captivatingly scented bulb plant from woodland environments; spreads by rhizomatous runners; striking red fruits; warning: the whole plant is poisonous!
Dryas spp.	Mountain avens	10–15cm (4–6in)	Late spring to early summer White	Sunny Dry, chalky or gravelly soil	Easily managed bedding plant with evergreen leathery grey-green foliage; nodding anemone-like flowers; attractive feathery seedheads.
Euphorbia cyparissias	Cypress spurge	30cm (12in)	Late spring Yellow-green	Sunny Normal soil	Spreading rhizomatous herbaceous perennial with feathery bluish-green leaves, that turn yellow in autumn; can be invasive.
Euphorbia polychroma		40cm (16in)	Mid-spring to early summer Yellow-green	Sunny to partially shady Normal to chalky soil	Attractive, decoratively leaved herbaceous perennial with striking flowers; does not spread; poisonous!; orange-red autumn colouring; all euphorbias can produce unpleasant skin reactions when touched so wear gloves when planting and tending.
Fragaria vesca	Wild strawberry	10–20cm (4–8in)	Mid- to late spring White	Sunny to partially shady Soil with humus	Native forest strawberry from woodland environments; spreads with runners; interesting varieties available with different-coloured foliage; fruity fragrance.
Galium odoratum	Sweet woodruff	10–20cm (4–8in)	Late spring to early summer White	Partially shady to shady Soil with humus	Native woodland herbaceous perennial which quickly spreads; leaves release the typically intense sweet woodruff scent when walked upon or crushed.

Botanical name	Common name	Height	Flowers	Situation	Notes
Gypsophila repens		10cm (4in)	Late spring to midsummer White	Sunny Dry, chalky or gravelly soil	Herbaceous perennial native to alpine regions; very floriferous; creates large mat-like areas.
Iberis sempervirens	Candytuft	15–30cm (6–12in)	Mid-spring to early summer White	Sunny to partially shady Normal soil	Evergreen subshrub with oblong, dark green leaves; regular pruning required at least every three years.
Iris hybrids	Bearded iris	15–35cm (6–14in)	Mid- to late spring Many colours	Sunny Normal soil	Delightful spring flowers with enduring attractive foliage; does not spread, so good for combining with other herbaceous perennials or bulbs.
Leptinella potentilloides	Brass buttons	5cm (2in)	Late spring to early summer Unassuming	Sunny to partially shady, normal soil	Forms dense grassy carpets but combines well with bulb plants; olive-coloured foliage, striking brown colour in winter; slight honeyed scent.
Mentha x piperita f. citrata	Lemon mint	30–90cm (12–36in) (depending on variety)	Late summer Lilac	Partially shady to sunny Poor, moist soil	Numerous varieties offer a real explosion of aromas, for example lemon mint, orange mint or eau de Cologne mint; the plants should be replanted every couple of years.
Nepeta x faassenii	Catmint	25–30cm (10–12in)	Late spring to early autumn Lavender-blue	Sunny Normal soil	Continuously flowering with greyish foliage; will flower again after pruning.
Nepeta racemosa	Catmint	25cm (10in)	Mid-spring to early autumn Lavender-blue	Sunny Normal soil	Leaves wider than *N. x faassenii*; grows well; sets copious amounts of seed when dry; leaves have a minty aroma.
Oenothera macrocarpa	Ozark sundrops	20–30cm (8–12in)	Summer Yellow	Sunny Gravelly or chalky soil	Continuously flowering with brilliant yellow blooms that open in the evening; narrow leaves with a white underside; occasional pruning required; flowers exude fragrance.
Prunella grandiflora	Large self-heal	20cm (8in)	Summer Crimson	Sunny to partially shady Rather dry soil, rich in nutrients	Undemanding, heavily and continuously flowering bedding plant; excellent for groundcover and attractive to bees; varieties with white, carmine-pink or violet flowers.
Sagina subulata	Pearlwort	5cm (2in)	Early to midsummer White	Sunny to partially shady Gravelly or chalky soil	The ideal substitute for grass in gaps! Moss-like herbaceous perennial that creates dense mats.
Saponaria x lempergii	Soapwort	20–25cm (8–10in)	Midsummer to early autumn Pink	Sunny Normal soil	Robust, and continually flowering; creates large cushions; prized for its late flowering time.

Planting in the Gaps

Botanical name	Common name	Height	Flowers	Situation	Notes
Sedum spp.	Stonecrop	5–15cm (2–6in)	Summer White, yellow, pink, carmine	Sunny Gravelly or poor soil	Effective bedding plant with numerous species and varieties, creates grass-, carpet- and cushion-like coverings; some evergreen; small star-shaped flowers.
Sempervivum spp.	Houseleek	10–20cm (4–8in)	Summer Pink	Sunny Gravelly or poor soil	Rosette-shaped herbaceous perennial with many different shapes and fleshy, evergreen leaves in various colours; exceptionally decorative and long-lived.
Thymus spp.	Thyme	5–40cm (2–16in) (depending on species and variety)	Late spring to Summer Pink	Sunny Warm, dry soil	Among the species and varieties of thyme there are different aromas, including lemon and orange thyme; low-growing, creeping species are often referred to as creeping thyme.
Viola cornuta	Horned violet	15cm (6in)	Spring to summer Dark blue	Sunny to partially shady Normal or stony soil	Spreading rhizomatous, evergreen perennial; in harsher locations winter protection may be required.

Walls

Dry stone walls are among the most attractive and interesting garden features. They are made from hewn stone blocks placed in layers without any mortar or other means of fixing and will last for a long time. For a dry stone wall to act as a retaining wall, a few rules must be followed:

▷ Make sure that about one third of the wall consists of tie stones. These are wide (or deep) stones that span the depth of the entire wall and create stability. Tie stones are not put in lengthways like the courses that make up the other two thirds of the wall but rather they have their longest edge at right angles to the front of the wall. Their length must be 1.5 times their height.

▷ Backfill the entire height of the wall with rubble or gravel.

▷ On sloping areas, provide a drainage system to carry away any water that would otherwise collect and cause problems.

▷ Lay a ballast foundation to a depth of 40–50cm (16–20in) and make it extend 10cm (4in) beyond each side of the first row of stones. The soil itself underneath also needs to be well compacted to provide the necessary stability.

▷ Make all joints as close-fitting as possible.

▷ Use the largest stones at the bottom and, generally, it is best to ensure they decrease in size towards the top.

▷ Lay the top of the wall with large cap stones, at least 40cm (16in) long, in order to create the required stability.

▷ Make sure that the stones are arranged so that the wall has a batter of 10–25 per cent; that is, it leans backwards in the direction of the slope and the stones tip slightly backwards.

▷ Arrange the joints to be staggered both vertically and horizontally so that the wall gains in strength and stability. The vertical joints should change every other layer.

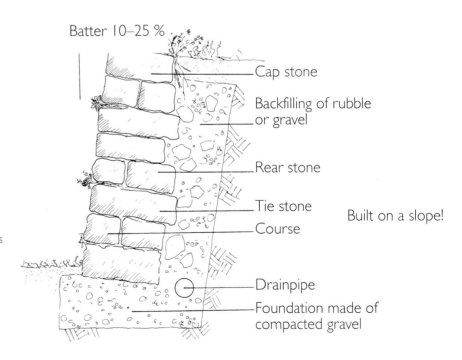

Batter 10–25 %

- Cap stone
- Backfilling of rubble or gravel
- Rear stone
- Tie stone
- Course
- Drainpipe
- Foundation made of compacted gravel

Built on a slope!

Cross-section of a dry stone wall. *If you intend to grow plants in the gaps, it is easier to plant these as the wall goes up as this will enable you to work sufficient soil in with them. Planting once the wall is finished requires considerably more effort.*

Surfaces

The hidden qualities of a surface lie in its structure – that is a properly prepared and level foundation of sufficient density to provide adequate frost-resistance and cope with the load-bearing layers on top. The surface can be simple or complicated in appearance, depending on the materials you choose and the pattern they are laid in.

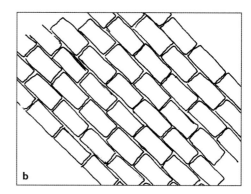

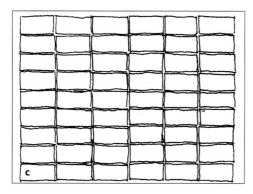

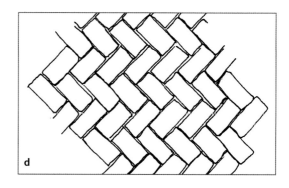

Laying patterns for bricks, slabs and paving:
a. *Rows or stretcher bond patterns are commonly used for laying bricks and paving slabs. Laid parallel to its direction of travel, they make a path seem longer and ensure that it can curve easily without any obvious changes in direction. Laid crossways, they will make it seem shorter, but still allow for neat changes in direction.*
b. *Laid diagonally to the direction of a travel, bricks and pavers can make a path look shorter. In* addition to its visual appeal, the advantage of a *diagonally-laid pattern is that it creates a surface that is capable of bearing high loads. It is useful for paths or driveways that have a lot of traffic.*
c. *Cross bonding is only suitable for surfaces that do not have to withstand heavy loads. To look truly impressive, great care is required when this type of pattern is laid so that all the joints line up, any unevenness is very obvious.*
d. *Equally decorative and very strong is the* herringbone pattern. This is one of the classic laying *techniques for bricks.*
e. *An old irregular laying technique for natural stone paving. Sadly, this beautiful loose pattern is very rare nowadays.*
f. *Natural stone slabs can also be laid in the unattractively named crazy paving style. Their visual appeal is their lack of direction, and they particularly suit gardens that are informal or more natural in appearance.*

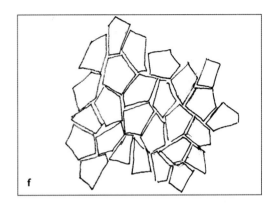

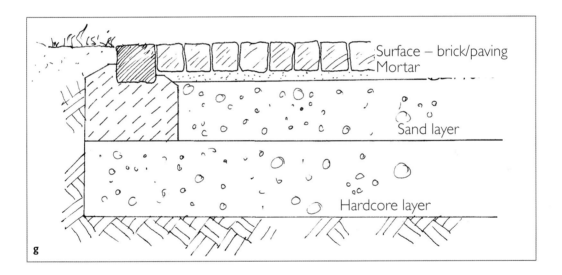

g. One of the best ways to lay paths and patios is to put down a layer of hardcore (100m/4in or more) followed by a layer of sand (50mm/2in or more). Both should be tamped down well and should be laid on compacted soil underneath. The method of fixing the top surface will vary according to the type you chose. Pavers can be fixed with a layer of dry mortar or with dabs of wet mortar placed for each slab. The gaps will need mortar joints. Surfaces, such as driveways, that are subject to a lot of traffic should also have a suitably stable edging or kerb.

Steps

Steps make walking up or down steep slopes – those with a gradient of 10 per cent or more – considerably easier and more pleasant.

Use the following guidelines to design your steps and find the appropriate tread/riser ratio.

▷ For outside steps the height of each riser should be a minimum of 10cm (4in) and maximum of 16cm (6in). A 38cm (15in) tread and a 15cm (6in) riser is a comfortable combination, recommended by most landscape architects.

▷ Choose either the tread or the riser dimensions first, depending on the style of the steps you require and its users.

▷ To calculate the tread/riser ratio, use the following equation:

tread + 2 x riser = 65–68cm (26–27in)

▷ When choosing a tread/riser ratio, consider the rise and run of the slope but do not try to make the ratio fit the slope. Doing so can cause a poor tread-to-riser relationship.

Common ratios are 15cm (6in) rise to 34cm (14in) thread or 16cm (6in) to 32cm (12½in).

▷ Steps require a foundation. A thick compressed gravel foundation of 20–30cm (8–12in) is sufficient for short flights of about four steps. With longer steps, a hardcore foundation is necessary.

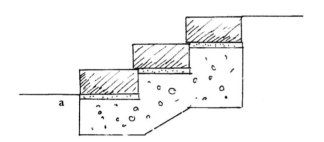

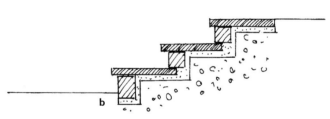

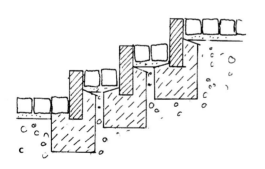

Cross-sections of the three types of steps. *Here are three basic types of step: block steps (a), flagstone steps (b) and riser steps (c). Without doubt, the most stable version is the block step; flagstone steps are not as strong. Riser steps are relatively inexpensive and are best for flights of steps on less-used paths. An adequate* *foundation is important for all these steps. If there are more than four steps, the foundation needs to be below the frost line, which will vary according to the region you live in. It is usually enough, though, if only the first and last step of the flight have a frost-free foundation.*

Glossary

accent plant - Any plant that is used to draw the eye in a bed or border or in a container. Accents might be created with tall plants in a mostly low-growing border or a spreading plant on an otherwise unadorned lawn.

annual - A plant that grows, flowers, produces seed and dies in one growing season - spring to autumn or winter. Some plants that cannot survive frosty weather without protection, such as busy lizzies, are often grown as annuals and then discarded, even though they could survive for many more years.

architectural plant - A plant with a striking shape, such as a weeping tree, or an interesting leaf form, such as spiky or huge and glossy. Architectural plants are often used for accents.

bedding plant - Usually annuals, grown for their flowers or attractive foliage, bedding plants are used en masse to create a vivid but short-lived display. Although they are associated with large flowerbeds, such as those in municipal parks, they can be used successfully in private gardens, too. Common bedding plants are primulas and wallflowers in spring plantings and salvias and canna lilies in summer displays.

biennial - A plant that survives two years, growing in the first year and producing flowers and seeds in the following year before dying. Some plants, such as wallflowers, are grown as biennials, even though they are capable of living for longer.

bulb - A bulb is a storage organ, usually underground, from which a plant can grow. Bulbs are made up of numerous leaves or leaf-like structures wrapped around each other and getting smaller towards the bulb centre. Onions and daffodils are bulbs.

compost - vegetative material from the kitchen and garden that is rotted down and then used to improve the quality of all soils. A good compost heap is made of a mixture of coarse material, such as vegetable peelings and green stems, and finer material, such as grass clippings and seedling weeds. Good compost is virtually odourless or smells quite pleasant. Always mix grass clippings in well with other material to prevent them clumping together in a smelly mass.

corm - Like a bulb, a corm is a storage organ like a squashed fleshy stem from which a plant can grow. Cyclamen, crocuses and montbretia are corms.

crown - Herbaceous perennials die down to a crown and roots in the winter. The crown is the cluster of dormant buds at the soil surface that will produce the next year's plant.

cultivar - A cultivar is a plant that varies in some way from the species to which it is related, perhaps having bigger flowers or being smaller or larger in growth. 'Cultivar' is short for 'cultivated variety'; cultivars are usually plants that have been deliberately bred or selected in gardens or nurseries. For example, the cultivar *Salvia patens* 'Cambridge Blue' has pale blue flowers, whereas those of the species, *Salvia patens*, are rich dark blue.

evergreen - An evergreen plant is one that is never without leaves at any point in the year. Perennials, shrubs and trees can all be evergreen.

fleece - Thin horticultural sheeting used to protect seedlings and frost-vulnerable plants.

formal garden - Any garden that has a strong structure and repeated shapes. Formal gardens are usually kept extremely neat and tidy. Formality can be created with patterned layouts, such as knot gardens and parterres, clipped plant shapes, like box *(Buxus)* or other hedging, and strong architectural features, such as paths and walls, and so on.

framework - In a garden, the framework is the underlying structure, the evergreens, the deciduous trees and the paths and other features, that will be visible in some form all year round.

gazebo - From the Persian meaning a platform to view the moon, a gazebo is a an enclosed, roofed structure, such as a summerhouse, often circular or hexagonal, and usually intended for sitting beneath.

genus - A plant genus (for example *Geranium*) consists of a group of plants that share a number of characteristics, such as flower appearance, general leaf shape, root structure and so on. The plural form is genera.

graft - A graft is produced when a shoot or part of a shoot of one plant is joined to the roots of another. Grafts are common in fruit trees, such as apples, because they enable the breeder to ensure that a tree will grow strongly but be of a predictable size, such as dwarf or medium. Ornamentals, such as roses, may be grafted to produce a plant of a

Glossary

reasonable size more quickly than it would grow naturally on its own roots or to ensure that the plant grows more healthily than it would on its own roots.

herbaceous perennial - A non-woody plant that lives for two years or more, appearing from a rootstock in spring and dying down for winter.

humus - Well-rotted vegetative matter, such as leaf mould or garden compost, that bulks out the soil, increasing fertility and water retention.

hybrid - A hybrid plant occurs when two different plants are crossed, such as two species in the same genus or two species in different genera. Hybrids can occur in the wild but they are often the result of deliberate breeding to produce plants with improved characteristics to the naturally occuring forms.

informal garden - An informal garden is any garden that is not formal. Informal gardens can contain elements of formality, such as clipped hedges or straight-edged flowerbeds, but they usually lack any sort of uniformity and symmetry and are more free in their planting. Cottage gardens are generally informal.

mulch - A material used to cover bear soil to retain water and reduce weed growth. Mulches can be bark, compost, gravel, black plastic and so on.

marginal plant - Marginal plants are so named because their preferred growing conditions - moist or wet soil - are found on the margins of ponds and other water sources.

naturalize - Some plants, such as species daffodils, primroses and cyclamen, are wonderful for naturalizing, which means that they can be planted in areas where the soil is not usually cultivated, such as in grass, under trees or on banks, and allowed to spread more or less unchecked.

panorama - A wide, open view seen from one point.

parterre - A garden with formally arranged geometrical flowerbeds.

pergola - A rectangular or square garden structure consisting of an equal number of upright supports bearing long beams and a series of crossbeams. The structure creates a lightly shaded area or walkway and is often used as a support for climbing plants such as roses and clematis.

pleach - To intertwine branches, especially when making a hedge. With pleached avenues the lower branches are often also removed.

rhizome - A fleshy stem-like underground organ from which a plant can grow. Rhizomes often grow horizontally and are one of the means by which a plant spreads. Irises have rhizomes that often grow on the soil surface.

rill - A very thin stretch of water, often moving, as in a small brook. Ornamental rills, with straight, stone-line banks, are often found in formal gardens.

rootstock - This can refer to the roots of any plant but more usually is used to refer to the roots and crown of herbaceous perennials and the roots that are used in grafting.

soil pH - Some plants are very sensitive to the acidity or alkalinity of the soil, which is measured in a scale from pH1, very acid, to pH14, very alkaline; pH7 is neutral. Plants such as camellias and rhododendrons require an acid soil to grow well.

species - In each genus there is one or more species (for example *Geranium endressii*). These are individual plants that share all the same characteristics. Unlike a cultivar, a species is a distinct plant that has evolved in the wild and all its offspring look the same.

subspecies (ssp.) - These are plants within a species that vary in some way from what is regarded as the true type. They might be identical to the species but have hairier leaves, for example.

topiary - Trimming and training plants, such as box (*Buxus*) and yew (*Taxus*), into geometric and representative shapes, including orbs, spirals, pyramids, birds and animals. The trimmed plants themselves are also called topiary.

tuber - Like a bulb, a tuber is a storage organ, usually underground, from which a plant can grow. Potatoes and dahlias are tubers.

vista - In gardens, vistas are usually a view glimpsed at the end of a long narrow opening, such as an avenue of yew hedging with a statue or other focal point at the end.